Notre Histoire

The First Hundred Years of Haitian Independence

by Ghislain Gouraige, Jr.

ISBN: 979-8-9883494-0-2

Notre Histoire

The First Hundred Years
of Haitian Independence

This book is dedicated to the courageous and hopeful Haitian nation—most importantly to those ancestors who ensured our independence for the first hundred years. They sacrificed prosperity for freedom, and overcame obstacles far greater than those that confront our people today. Let us learn about what they have achieved and gather inspiration to create a united Haiti.

FOREWORD

by David Lawrence

I THOUGHT I knew Haiti.

Here I sit at my computer in my library at home, above me to the left an abundance of books I have read about Haiti. Some have been especially meaningful to me, beginning with *Masters of the Dew* by Jacques Roumain, 11 by Edwidge Danticat (my favorite being *The Farming of Bones)*, two biographies of Toussaint Louverture, *The Uses of Haiti* by Paul Farmer, *Who Owns Haiti* edited by Robert Maguire and Scott Freeman, and the list goes on.

As a publisher of the *Miami Herald,* I needed to understand the places from where so many of our readers came. Every single time I came back to Miami, I marveled how tall the people stood despite brutality, poverty and invariably inept governments.

One evening in 1997, by which time I had already been to Haiti multiple times, I was at a dinner table in Port-au-Prince that included the president of the republic and the American ambassador. There, with Haitian leaders who could make a difference, I was told that the nation's greatest need was high-quality education and skilled labor that could build a nation. In the years following, my friend, Monsignor Franklyn Casale, the president of St. Thomas University in Miami-Dade, and I raised a million dollars in South Florida to make the vision come to be. Successful at that, we were back in September 2001, on that most meaningful 9/11, to dedicate, Haiti Tec. At breakfast and on CNN we witnessed horror as jets commanded by terrorists ploughed into the World Trade Center. Two hours later, preceded by prayers led by the Monsignor, we dedicated a vocational-technical school so young Haitians could obtain sought-after skills—computers to construction—for the future of the republic. In the years since I have been to Haiti so many times to check how the school was doing, including after the devastating earthquake of 2010.

Over many years I read, traveled, asked questions, learned much—but had so much more to know and learn. Today I am better educated, and I thank Ghislain Gouraige and this book for that.

Yes, I knew that Haiti was the richest colony in the world, built off economic wickedness by French colonial plantation owners who mercilessly beat slaves to harvest the sugar cane and turn it into "white gold" that made so many fabulously wealthy. Yes, I knew of the revolt of slaves, the result being Haiti coming to be the hemisphere's second oldest republic since 1804—preceded only by the United States. Yes, I knew of the crippling debt on Haiti that the French insisted on. Yes, I knew that Haiti had about the same number of chiefs of state as the U.S., but with many of them assassinated or driven from office. Yes, I knew that one of America's greatest, Frederick Douglass, was our envoy to Haiti in the late 19th century. Yes, I knew that American Marines were dispatched to Haiti in 1915 to protect my own country's economic interests, thence to become the real and brutal power in Haiti for the next 19 years. Yes, I knew that FDR announced a "Good Neighbor" policy in the hemisphere, but we really weren't. Yes, I knew of the massacres of 1937. Yes, I knew how we propped up the despotism of Duvaliers.

Yet for all that, I had missed much I needed to know—indeed a whole century. Except for the first four years, all of the

19th century was missing for me. Bad things happened—good things happened too. I needed to know both. I found it in Ghislain Gouraige's superbly researched, well told "Notre Histoire: The First Hundred Years of Haitian Independence."

As the late and celebrated Paul Harvey would say: "Now here's the rest of the story."

—David Lawrence

GHISLAIN GOURAIGE, JR.

INTRODUCTION

Tʜɪs ʙooᴋ has been written for the members of the Haitian nation living abroad. We are also called the diaspora. As such we have been raised in other countries, US, Canada, Bahamas, France and elsewhere. We share a love for our country of origin or the country of our parents and grandparents. Those of us who are second or even third generation Haitians living abroad have not been taught the history of our country. What we have learned has come from the pen of authors who are not Haitian. For the most part Haitian authors have written in French and now in Creole. As such, those raised in English speaking countries have learned our history from non-native sources.

Those secondhand sources are not unbiased. They come to the topic of Haiti with an agenda. Their focus is on certain aspects of our long and varied history. They focus on the independence period, or on the occupation period. The more recent focus has been on the years of dictatorship, failed state and poverty. Of late, it is impossible for us to read about Haiti without being reminded that Haiti is the "poorest country in the Western Hemisphere." That refrain is constant and permeates the way that we are viewed.

This book will tell a different story. It will focus on the first hundred years of our independence. It will tell our history from our point of view, and in a manner that helps our current generation better understand the obstacles that had to be overcome for Haiti to remain independent into the 20th century. Those who have never given thought to what the young nation faced, will learn about the proud and brave men and women who maintained our freedom after it was secured.

This is the story that will be recounted here. Those of us who live abroad have not been taught this story from the perspective of Haitians. This story is also meant to remind those of us who may despair at the current state of affairs to maintain hope. We have overcome obstacles far greater than those that confront us today. Our ancestors achieved something that has never been repeated. A slave rebellion that led to the founding of an independent nation.

In this book we will tell the story of how that nation remained independent. The great leaders and courageous people who had to make sacrifices and endured a great deal to stay a free nation. No other country faced the daunting odds that confronted the generations that followed the authors of our independence. This is their story and ours.

GHISLAIN GOURAIGE, JR.

AUTHOR'S NOTE

THERE ARE approximately 3.5 million Haitians living abroad, and there are 11 million people living in the physical boundaries of the Republic of Haiti. That one third of Haitians has come to be known as the diaspora. This is the term used to describe the overseas part of Haiti that constitutes an important part of the Haitian nation. The remittances sent by diaspora Haitians helps keep the economy of the country afloat. Visits from diaspora make up the majority of the tourist industry. In fact, the contribution of the diaspora has become so noteworthy that the government established a separate ministry to deal with diaspora affairs. The ministry caters to what is officially referred to as the 10th department. Overseas Haitians are fully recognized as part and parcel of the Haitian nation.

The successes of the diaspora are celebrated by all. Naomi Osaka became the number one ranked woman in tennis. Haitan-Canadian author, Dany Laferrière joined France's literary greats in the Academie Française.[1,2] Michaelle Jean was Governor General of Canada. Claudine Fay was named the 30th président of Harvard University. Haitians the world over take pride in these achievements as a source of pride and uplift for the nation. The boat people who came to the U.S. unable to read and write are sending their kids to college. The number of doctors, nurses, engineers, lawyers and other professional designations obtained by the diaspora is impressive.

The world looks upon Haiti and sees a poor country with severely depleted natural resources. A fractured political entity with a difficult path ahead. That is one narrative and unfortunately it is the only one being told. There is quite another story. Our story, the one about our people and nation. The one where we have overcome tremendous odds to find success outside of our homeland. The one where we have not turned

---

1. HAITIAN-CANADIAN (QUEBEQOUIS) AUTHOR AND VICTIM OF DIASPORA; Britannica, T. Editors of Encyclopaedia. "Dany Laferrière." *Encyclopedia Britannica,* April 9, 2022. https://www.britannica.com/biography/Dany-Laferriere.

2. CREATED BY RICHELIEU IN 1934. MEMBERS INCLUDE THE BEST OF FRENCH LITERATURE IN THE LAST 400 YRS. Britannica, T. Editors of Encyclopaedia. "French Academy." *Encyclopedia Britannica,* March 29, 2018. https://www.britannica.com/topic/French-Academy.

our backs on our people. The one where the Haitian nation stands together to build a better tomorrow. The one where our people are our most valued natural resource.

This is the story that we need to tell ourselves. We need to change the narrative about the Haitian people. Our nation doesn't only reside within the physical boundaries of the Republic of Haiti. Our nation and people exist all around the world and continue to achieve great things. We are indeed worthy of our ancestors and the sacrifices they made to forge us into one nation and one people. The story that we tell ourselves is quite different.

1

OUR FOREBEARERS

ST. DOMINGUE was the wealthiest colony in the world.[3] Pirates and flibustiers used the western third of Hispaniola as a base to raid the ships of the Spaniards. Over time they settled and operated under the flag, protection and oversight of France. French planters soon followed, looking to strike it rich quick. But it wasn't the Europeans who made the island what it was, no matter what they told themselves.

Long before the pirates and planters, Ayiti (the name given by the original inhabitants) was a paradise on earth. The indigenous Arawak had a thriving culture and traded with

---

3. James C. L. R. 1963. *The Black Jacobins : Toussaint L'ouverture and the San Domingo Revolution* Second edition revised ed. New York: Vintage Books.

the other islands,[4] but were in no way prepared for what was to come when Columbus came ashore. This earthly paradise was named Hispaniola (little Spain) by Columbus. To this day the island which is shared by two nations bears the name Hispaniola. Before Columbus our island was called Quisqueya (cradle of life) and Ayiti by the first inhabitants. Ayiti (the western third) means land of mountains.

We Haitians consider the Arawaks among our forefathers. From them we learned about the land, the plants, fruits and fauna. To this day we use many of their words in our local language to describe the plants, animals and places.[5] Here are some familiar names from food: *cassave,* to names of cities: *goaves* (as in the cities of Grand and Ti Goaves). The predator cayman; just to list a few. Our language, food and culture still bear the traces of our Arawak forbearers. Our deep attachment to the land comes in part from them.

We suffer as we recall their decimation by disease, and genocide. It is not a coincidence that we named our country using the name of the original inhabitants. The army of independence flew their colors in our early flags. We are

---

4. Tennesen, Michael. "Uncovering the Arawaks." *Archaeology* 63, no. 5 (2010): 51–56. http://www.jstor.org/stable/41780608.

5. Fouchard, Jean. "Regards sur Le Temps Passé. *Langue et Littérature des Aborigènes D'Ayiti.*

their children in spirit. To understand Haitians one needs to know that we flow from them. For us the link is direct. We would never have survived but for them. The marrons escaped to the remote interior to join and be sheltered by the Arawak remnants.

Among the more famous of our Arawak forbearers we celebrate is Anacaona; the warrior queen who fought the Spaniards. She lives on in our mythology. We avenged her and all of those who fought alongside her and lost to Spain. Caonabo was the Cacique who loved and fought alongside Anacaona. Theirs is among the love stories that animate our past and fire our imaginations. The Cacique Henry fought and defeated the Spaniards. He carved out for his people autonomy from Spain and moved his people to the remote, mountainous region of Quisqueya.

In the story we tell, some Arawak survived in those remote locations that were of little interest to the Spaniards who focused their attention on the eastern side of the island. When reading the history books about the demise of the Arawak we are told that they died and disappeared. In our story, we recognize that a small number survived in the of the western third of the island. They ran away to Ayiti where the Spaniards would not follow.

We believe that by the time that the French took over the western third of the island after the Treaty of Ryswick in 1697 some remnants of the Arawak remained.[6] The French colony that became St. Domingue focused the settlements on the coast. The cities that were founded were coastal with the idea of exporting the riches of the colony back to the metropole. Hence no one paid attention to the remote and inaccessible mountains of the interior. Resources were not wasted on the vast interior range of mountains that define Haiti. The French settled on the coast and cultivated the fertile lands in the valleys

At this point, there was no proof of the existence of our Arawak forefathers. We do know that when the enslaved ran away, they fled to the mountains of the interior. The "Negres Marrons" as they were called lived in organized villages in areas so remote that the French could not find them. We believe that these marrons were guided and helped by the surviving Arawak. They taught these marrons about the fauna and terrain. Somehow the marrons learned the medicinal properties of plants, and which fruits were edible. They learned not only how to survive but to thrive.

---

6. Britannica, T. Editors of Encyclopaedia. "Hispaniola." *Encyclopedia Britannica,* September 30, 2022. https://www.britannica.com/place/Hispaniola.

The names of places, plants, and animals all carry the names given them by the Arawak, not a Spanish or French equivalent. Those Arawak who managed to survive became one with us.[7]

The enslaved of St. Domingue knew that by escaping to the mountains far from the shore that they could find refuge. In fact, they did. The numbers are not easy to ascertain; no records were kept. But the existence of that population is not buried deep within our psyche. In fact, the population of the southern part of the country has a different hue and speaks with a different accent. The same words are pronounced with a softer tongue that we think resembles the way our Arawak forefathers spoke.[8]

The indigenous religion known as *vaudou* is primarily African in origin. Yet in the south of Haiti there is form of *vaudou* called Champuelle that bears certain aspects of the Arawak religion.[9] The Arawak influence is spiritual and we carry that with us in the religion. The celebrations for carnival have always featured the first inhabitants who have left their mark on the culture, religion and history of Haiti.

---

7. Moreau de Saint-Mery, Médéric Louis Élie (1996). "The Border Maroons of Saint Domingue." In Price, Richard (ed.). *Maroon Societies: Rebel Slave Communities in the Americas.* Baltimore: Johns Hopkins University Press.

8. Fouchard, Jean. *Regards sur Le Temps Passé. Langue et Littérature des Aborigènes D'Ayiti.*

9. Corbett, Bob (1995) Retrieved November 20, 2018.

In our day and age, it is interesting to see how some of our neighbors in the Caribbean look to reclaim their history as descendants of the Tainos (and Arawak). Our country bears the name that the Arawak gave to the land. Our people never severed the links. We see ourselves as their direct descendants.

2

ST. DOMINGUE

THE FRENCH COLONY of St. Domingue rapidly became the richest of France's colonial possessions, in time the world's largest producer of both sugar and coffee. It was perhaps the wealthiest colony of any of the major European powers.[10] Many French aristocrats went to St. Domingue to create their fortune. The fabulous wealth obtained in St. Domingue could allow one to obtain a noble title. The wealth of St. Domingue was the stuff of legend in France. The colony produced sugar, coffee, cacao among its main exports to France where the demand for these raw materials was insatiable. Ever larger plantations were created to meet the increased demand.

---

10. Britannica, T. Editors of Encyclopaedia. "Hispaniola." *Encyclopedia Britannica,* September 30, 2022. https://www.britannica.com/place/Hispaniola.

From an economic perspective, making it rich quick would mean exploiting the enslaved. The slave trade met the demand for labor and enslaved Africans from such areas as the Gulf of Guinea, and the kingdoms of Dahomey, Benin, and Kongo. Enslaved Africans were put to work in the plantations of St. Domingue, and then tirelessly and mercilessly exploited. So much so that a Code Noir[11] was instituted. This royal edict set limits on the way the enslavers could treat those that they enslaved. But the Code Noir was widely ignored by planters. The distance from the metropole left the enslavers in control. Moreover, local administrators had little appetite to enforce those laws.

Consequently, the system in St. Domingue created a boiling pot of resentment. The vast majority of those who lived in St. Domingue were the enslaved. The strict social hierarchy had Grand Blancs (large plantation owners) at the top. The Petit Blancs (who worked for the planters and did not own land) rounded out the top of the social pyramid. The next level was reserved for the *mulâtres* who were the children of the planters and the enslaved.[12] Some of the *gens de couleur* or *mulâtres* (the

---

11. "Liceo Cantonale di Locarno." Archived from the original on 4 March 2007.

12. King, Stewart (2001). *Blue Coat or Powdered Wig: Free People of Color in Pre-Revolutionary Saint Domingue.* Athens, Georgia: University of Georgia Press. p.44.13

terms are interchangeable) inherited the plantations including enslaved from their fathers.

Notwithstanding the fact that a number of the *mulâtres* were wealthy, and even sometimes as much as the Grand Blancs, they were treated as a socially inferior class. The French of St. Domingue came up with a plethora of descriptions and adjectives to distinguish the *mulâtres* from the *negres*. At the next level of the social ladder were the emancipated Africans who lived in the cities and were not a part of the plantation system. At the bottom were the enslaved living in misery and mistreated.

We cannot say with certainty that the planter class of St. Domingue was more odious in their exploitation of the enslaved than their neighbors in Cuba, or the southern U.S. What is burnished in the minds of all Haitians is that the conditions to which the enslaved were treated was unsustainable. The cruelty and brutality of the system could not endure. Most importantly, the enslaved vowed to bear it no longer.

The economy of the sugar plantations lent itself to a system where the labor of the enslaved was the secret sauce to the recipe for success. Large amounts of labor input was needed to plant, and harvest the sugar crop. In addition, the processing of the cane into refined sugar ready for export also required great labor. The cost of labor was negligible; hence all was skewed towards having even more enslaved. Mass production of the sugar done so cheaply came to have huge implications for the plantations of St. Domingue.

More male enslaved were needed than women to perform the backbreaking labor required. The number of hours needed during the harvest was close to 20 hours per day. The enslaved were poorly nourished as a way to control expenses. The need to replace those who were less productive was paramount. All these factors and more created a system in St. Domingue where the colony's demographics were influenced by the production of sugar. Consequently, the number of enslaved represented nearly 90% of the total population of the colony. If ever there were to be a serious revolt, the sheer weight of the numbers would operate against the planters and their overseers.

Many of the wealthiest planters preferred to reside in Paris and enjoy the fabulous wealth generated by their colonial possessions. Running the plantation was often left to overseers who were considered the Petit Blancs within the strict hierarchy of St. Domingue. The overseers were held to ambitious production goals and permitted to do whatever was necessary to get results.

The Code Noir[13] set forth how the enslaved were to be treated. Limits were set on the autonomy of the enslavers over the enslaved. But hardly anyone in St. Domingue paid attention to the Code Noir, much less seeking to enforce its restrictions on the planters. The planters were unrestricted in their power over the enslaved. They enjoyed a lifestyle unmatched elsewhere, their every whim and fancy catered to. This exercise of absolute power with no accountability created every incentive needed for those with a cruel disposition to give vent to their basest desires.

The slave system practiced in St. Domingue was cruel and inhumane; a fact burnished in our collective psyches.[14] The rebellion, revolt and the ensuing atrocities are not divorced from that reality. The enslaved had had enough and were looking for the opportunity to exact their revenge.

____

13. *Liceo Cantonale di Locarno.* Archived from the original on 4 March 2007.

14. Palmer, Vernon Valentine (1996). "The Origins and Authors of the Code Noir." *Louisiana Law Review.* 56: 363–408.

3

NEGRES MARRONS

THE EUROPEAN COLONISTS tended to concentrate settlements and ultimately, cities on the coasts of Santo Domingo and St Domingue. In the northern part of St. Domingue, Cap Français was the largest city. A port city, it became known as the "Paris of the Caribbean." It was well situated for trade with France and ports in the region. In the western part of St. Domingue, Port-au-Prince was the main city on the coast. The south had Jacmel as its dominant port and city.

Economic activity was focused around these ports of call. The large plantations were located in the regions adjacent to coastal centers. The valleys and plains surrounding these cities produced bountiful harvests. The Plaine du Nord and the Artibonite valley were vital to the economic health of the colony.[15]

The interior of the island, full of mountains and hills, was relatively unpopulated. The runaway enslaved, the Marrons, found refuge in the remote interior. The unique geography of the western third of Hispaniola provided ample remote locations for the Marrons to escape. Once freed the Marrons found others like them. They founded settlements, knowing they would not be hunted down or brought back to slavery.

It is well known that the Marrons established fortified locations both remote and impregnable. In fact, there are no recorded instances where the French reached these settlements, conquered the Marrons and then brought them back to the plantations. The Negre Marrons were courageous rebels who had enough of slavery and took matters into their own hands. They preferred to flee and tempt fate. What they found was freedom from slavery. But the Negres Marrons didn't just escape never to be heard from again. Quite the opposite.

The Negres Marrons are legendary in Haitian history. What the cowboy and gaucho represent to the U.S. and Argentina

---

15. Knight, Franklin W.; Liss, Peggy K. (1991). *Atlantic Port Cities: Economy, Culture, and Society in the Atlantic World, 1650–1850.* p. 91.

folklore, the Marron is the equivalent is Haitian lore. The Marron was a renegade who sought and gained freedom. Once free, they conspired to subvert the slave system. The Marrons contacted the enslaved on the plantations and plotted to exact revenge on planters. They inspired the enslaved and were a scourge to the enslavers.

Mackandal was such a Marron. He was said to have had an accident with sugar cane machinery leaving him with a mangled hand. Given less back breaking work, he escaped into the mountains. We celebrate him because he was among those who did not forget those he had left behind. Instead, he conspired with them and maintained a network that encompassed the northern part of the colony. Organized and training a group of other Marrons, he led an ambitious conspiracy to poison the water supplies of Cap Français and thus be rid of the enslavers. He was betrayed, caught (the mangled hand confirmed his identity) and ultimately burned at the stake.[16]

Mackandal left us a legacy of resistance to slavery and the hunger to put an end to the pernicious institution. In death he was not forgotten. He is celebrated as one who escaped,

---

16. Courtin, Sebastien Jacques (1758). Mémoire sommaire sur les pratiques magiques et empoisonnements prouvés aux procès instruits et jugés au Cap contre plusieurs Nègres et Négresses dont le chef, nommé François Macandal, a été condamné au feu et exécuté le vingt janvier 1758. A.N. COLONIES. p. 88.

found freedom and then organized followers to put an end to slavery.

What captured the imagination about the Marrons is that they gained freedom by running away, and not forgetting those left behind. They never settled for their own personal freedom. What is embedded in the deep recesses of our collective memory is that they sought to exterminate the enslavers. They posed a threat, but the enslavers could not eradicate them. Their numbers continued to grow, and they were to be heard from on the march to our independence.

4

BOIS CAIMAN

Boukman[17] is another name that rolls off the tongue. Born in Jamaica and brought to St. Domingue, he was tall, charismatic and physically very strong. A vaudou priest, he generated fierce loyalty among his followers.

Boukman organized a ceremony at the Bois Caiman near the Morne Rouge on August 14, 1791.[18] That fateful night, forever changed our history. A large number of enslaved from a number of plantations gathered for a ceremony. They witnessed an outburst of thunder and lightning whose force and

---

17. Dorsainvil, Dr. J. C. "Manuel Histoire D'Haiti" Editions Henri Deschamps; Portus Principis, 15 July 1934

18. Geggus, David Patrick (2002). Haitian revolutionary studies. Indiana: Indiana University Press. p. 72.

violence foreshadowed something great. It was as if the sky opened and the ground groaned. The wind lashed fiercely, and the rain poured. Trees were felled and their branches strewn.

Amidst this turmoil, the vaudou priestess, Cécile Fatiman,[19] appeared and captured everyone's attention. She was possessed. Her body was contorted and shook violently. She began to chant and dance, whirling about and holding a knife. Those in attendance were spellbound. A black pig was brought forward and the priestess plunged her knife into the animal and cut its throat. The blood flowed and each in attendance drank from that sacrificial pig. They pledged themselves to follow Boukman. The stage was set, there would be no turning back. [20,21]

St. Domingue had never seen such a moment before or since. As planned by Boukman and his supporters, the enslaved on several plantations rose up as one.[22] On the night of August 22nd 1791, the enslaved erupted in insurrection,

---

19. Joan Dayan, *Haiti, History, and the Gods,* University of California Press, 1998

20. Elizabeth McAlister. "From Slave Revolt to a Blood Pact with Satan: The Evangelical Rewriting of Haitian History" Studies in Religion/Sciences Religieuses 41.2 (2012). Available at: http://works.bepress.com/elizabeth_mcalister/37

21. Thylefors, Markel (March 2009) "'Our Government is in Bwa Kayiman:' a Vodou Ceremony in 1791 and its Contemporary Signifcations" Archived 22 July 2012 at the Wayback Machine Stockholm Review of Latin American Studies, Issue No. 4

22. Geggus, David Patrick (2002). *Haitian Revolutionary Studies.* Indiana: Indiana University Press. p. 72.

something that the enslavers had not anticipated, yet long feared. It was time to take revenge for all those years of oppression and suffering. Passion and rage took over; few were spared, even women and children.

They were avenging themselves for what they had suffered and for those who did not survive the passage to St. Domingue on those miserable ships where they were herded like cattle. They were also avenging those who could not survive the work demanded of them by the sugar plantation economy. They avenged those who succumbed to the enslavers and died in humiliation and degradation. We were treated as sub-human and responded in kind.

The massacres, savage and much criticized by the rest of the world, brought fear and terror to enslavers throughout the Americas. The slave system in Cuba and the U.S. South trembled at the thought that this could happen. We care not what enslavers have written about us and our insurrection. Those who wronged the enslaved of St. Domingue were going to pay with their lives for what they had done. There were individual acts of kindness toward those enslavers who were well liked. They were brought to safety.

We do not kid ourselves nor have we shied away from the brutality of the insurrection. The enraged rebelled and burned, ravaged, killed and set out to destroy all vestiges of slavery. Plantations were set ablaze and the whole Plaine du Nord was aflame.

Boukman was the principal leader, accompanied by other Marrons such as Jean-Francois, Jeannot, and Biassou. Boukman's authority was absolute, and his orders were followed without question. The rebels were briefly in command of much of the North. The enslavers were in shock, fearful and had not yet regrouped.

Eventually, the uprising was put down, and Boukman was felled while fighting. He was always at the head of his men who thought him invincible. The rebels, poorly armed, were ultimately vanquished. Boukman's head was displayed on a pike in a public place in Cap-Français as a trophy as well as a warning to those who would try to copy him.[23]

Even Boukman's death did not put an immediate end to the insurrection. Leaders such as Jean-Francois and Biassou still in controlled territory and were not prepared to relinquish hard-won gains. To regain control over the colony the government of France sent forth commissioners appointed by the National Assembly to restore order in St. Domingue. These commissioners were given great powers to bring the situation under control.

____

23. 2007-08-26. Archived from the original on 2007-08-26. Retrieved 2019-12-04.

The story of the French Revolution has been told and retold many times. But it is worth remembering that there were Jacobins among the Assembly who took the notion of *liberté, egalité et fraternité* to its logical conclusion and came to oppose slavery as against the ideals of the revolution.[24] These men of integrity and morality represented for us the best that the French revolution had to offer. Among those men was a commissioner sent to St. Domingue by the National Assembly: Sonthonax.

He decreed an end to slavery in St. Domingue. His motivation was part revolutionary fervor as well as a practical realization that he needed the enslaved on his side. Before being sent to St. Domingue he had written that St. Domingue should belong to the Blacks who had earned it by the sweat of their brow.

The French Revolution was an epochal event that threatened the established order of the European world. The continental powers went to war with France. Thus, both the British and Spanish threatened St. Domingue. The British invaded by sea and the Spaniards from the east in Santo Domingo. The Spanish recruited the Marrons and their leaders to fight

---

24. Cleves, Rachel Hope. "'Jacobins in This Country': The United States, Great Britain, and Trans-Atlantic Anti-Jacobinism." *Early American Studies* 8, no. 2 (2010): 410–45.

alongside them. These formerly enslaved who escaped into the remote mountains of St. Domingue were drafted into the army of Spain to fight against their former enslavers. These leaders with no allegiance to France, were prepared to negotiate the best deal for themselves. Jean-Francois, and Biassou joined forces with Spain.

Sonthonax going a step further, enlisted the support of the formerly enslaved to defeat the enemies of France.[25] The formerly enslaved were armed and took part in the defense of St. Domingue. Sonthonax told the newly freed citizens of St. Domingue that their arms guaranteed freedom. Whomsoever sought to take away their arms would also take their freedom. Truer words had not been spoken.

The National Assembly caught up in the rapture of its ideals make good on the promise of *liberté, egalité et fraternité.* Slavery was abolished in France and its colonies. For Haitians that cemented the glory of the revolution, France at its best, living up to the ideals it proclaimed to the world.

---

25. Sonthoax. 1797. *Review of Extrait Du Rapport Adresse Au Directoire Executif Par Le Citoyen Toussaint L'Ouverture.* Cap-Français: P. Roux, Imprimeur de la Comission.

5

TOUSSAINT

T HEN CAME TOUSSAINT.[26] In recent times Toussaint has been referred to as the Black Spartacus; he is also among those called Black Jacobins.[27, 28]Among those of African descent in the New World, none had risen to his lofty position. From slave to master. Those planters of St. Domingue were bowing to him and relying upon him to restore their fortunes. He became the master of the enslavers.

26. CLARKE, John Henrik. "Toussaint-Louverture and the Haitian Revolution" Présence Africaine, no. 89 (1974): 179–87.

27. James, C.L.R *The Black Jacobins*: Toussaint L'Ouverture and the San Domingo, London: Secker & Warburg (1938). Revised edition, New York: Vintage Books/Random House (1963).

28. Forsdick, Charles, and Christian Høgsbjerg. "The Harder They Come, The Harder They Fall…: 1801–03." In *Toussaint Louverture: A Black Jacobin in the Age of Revolutions*, 104–27. Pluto Press, 2017.

Until 2008 with the election of President Obama no other son or daughter of Africa had amassed such power and influence in the Western Hemisphere. He rose to heights that none could have imagined. Governor-General of the most prosperous colony of the world's mightiest nation. The armies he led defeated the French, Spanish and English in battle.

He was a military as well as political genius and a visionary, strategist and tactician. He always seemed to be a step ahead. His name L'Ouverture means the opening, or the path forward or even the way out. Time and again Toussaint found ways to outsmart and take advantage of his adversaries. He was indefatigable, an able horseman, Toussaint rode often for hours and days on end and appeared where none expected him. Tireless, he planned while others slept.

He wore out his aides with boundless energy. He would dictate several letters simultaneously to each of his secretaries, keeping track of all that in his head.

Toussaint was born, enslaved in 1743,[29] on the Habitation Breda where he spent the first 40 years of his life. He was the grandson of Gaou-Guinou who was king of the Aradas nation. In captivity, he learned how to read and write. A devoted

---

29. Dorsaninvil, Dr. J. C. "Manuel Histoire D'Haiti" Editions Henri Deschamps; Portus Principis, 15 July 1934

equestrian, he developed an endurance in the saddle that would serve him in later life.

By 1789 he was the confidant and right hand of the plantation's overseer.

Toussaint was among those who conspired to lead the rebellion in the plaine du Nord thus devastating plantations. He joined Biassou in 1791 as his main adviser and lieutenant. Along with Biassou, they were allied with Spain in its war against France. The officers of the Spanish army were quite impressed by his intelligence and capacity. Training him in the art of warfare, he became one of the most effective of Biassou's men. He rounded up and trained a band of Marrons that became a serviceable army of 3,000 men. Leading his men to battle, he defeated the French in several engagements. The Spaniards promoted him to the rank of Lieutenant-General. He was well on his way.

Toussaint's success gave rise to jealousy on the part of his leader Biassou. Jean-Francois and Biassou were the leaders of the Marrons with followers allied to Spain. They were given arms and training to forge an army to fight against France. Toussaint was a latecomer and fast rising star. They felt threatened by him, and in turn conspired against him. The Spaniards took no sides and let things play themselves out.

Biassou and Jean-François tried to assassinate Toussaint and failed.[30] They did however kill his youngest brother, Jean-Pierre who was at Toussaint's side. This led Toussaint to make a very difficult decision. He couldn't stay on the Spanish side and risk getting killed by his confreres. His other option was to ally with the British. Lastly, he could join France and drive both the Spaniards and British from St. Domingue. The path of least resistance was to join with the British, and given the weakened state of the French the riskiest option was to join France. Toussaint l'Ouverture was the man of destiny; the one to find the path, the way, the opening. He chose France.

Having chosen France, Toussaint had to do battle with his former chiefs Biassou and Jean-Francois[31] It took several campaigns and by the end of 1794 Toussaint led the French in the defeat of the Spaniards. With that done it remained to expel the English from St. Domingue. The English had expended considerable resources to gain a foothold in St. Domingue and weren't about to fold so easily. They tried every trick in the book so to speak. When bribery and the promise of honors

30. Dorsainvil, Dr. J. C. "Manuel Histoire D'Haiti" Editions Henri Deschamps; Portus Principis, 15 July 1934

31. Perry, James M. (2005). *Arrogant Armies: Great Military Disasters And The Generals Behind Them.* Castle Books Incorporated.

and promotions failed, they dug in and fought. In the end they too were defeated and driven from St. Domingue.

The armies of two European powers were repulsed and defeated. Toussaint rose to the rank of Brigadier General in the army of the Republic. His talent for organization and administration created a confluence of factors that allowed for those parts of St. Domingue under his control to thrive and prosper. The planters returned to their plantations and those formerly enslaved went back to work on the plantations as free men whose labor was compensated.

By 1798 Toussaint had accumulated greater influence and power until he became the supreme leader of St. Domingue.[32] In just 5 years, he rose to a supreme position by overcoming rivals and intrigue. First, there were the commissioners sent to St. Domingue by the French Assembly. Among them was Sonthonax who gave us the arms to defend ourselves and our liberty. Sonthonax outmaneuvered by Toussaint, was forced to leave St. Domingue.

Toussaint's most formidable rival was the mulâtre general Andre Rigaud who played an important role in defeating the

---

32. James, C.L.R. *The Black Jacobins: Toussaint L'Ouverture and the San Domingo,* London: Secker & Warburg (1938). Revised edition, New York: Vintage Books / Random House (1963).

Spaniards and English. Based in the South, he had a formidable army at his disposal. Rigaud was not prepared to strike a bargain with Toussaint. Conflict was then inevitable. This is a sad chapter in our history. The fighting was bloody. Toussaint was aided by his able generals Christophe and Dessalines. Rigaud was defeated and had to leave St. Domingue for France. Toussaint systematically eliminated Rigaud's supporters and mercilessly took control of St. Domingue. From that point forward he faced no further local opposition.

His next step was to take control of the entire island. Thus, in early 1801 he sent an army of 25,000 soldiers into Santo Domingo. The army was split in two with General Moyse attacking first, and the rest of the army led by Toussaint formed the second wave. Resistance was minimal, and Toussaint became the acknowledged ruler of the entire island. He regained all of St. Domingue, and in turn, the island for France. A position that France had never reached. France reigned over all of Hispaniola. Toussaint's first act was to proclaim liberty for all. Slavery was abolished.

This man of humble origins, enslaved for the first 50 or so years of his life, was transformed into the leader of France's most valued overseas possession. He surprised many by his talents as an administrator, dividing the island into several departments. His generals, responsible for governing in his name, comprised the executive branch. Strict discipline was maintained. Toussaint was in total control and sent the formerly enslaved back to work. He wanted the economy restarted and order maintained.

Toussaint convened a constitutional assembly to draft a constitution for St. Domingue. The constitution, duly approved by the assembly, in essence created an autonomous colony. Toussaint was named Governor General for life with the right to designate his successor. The all-powerful Toussaint governed with an iron hand. He brooked little dissent and operated with military discipline.

Toussaint was indefatigable, got by on little to no sleep, ate little and maintained total control of his faculties. He was always on the move, riding his horse to all parts of the island. At the most unexpected times he would appear and swoop down on unsuspecting civil servants who had caught his attention for some dereliction.

Notwithstanding all his talent and effort, Toussaint still had to contend with issues that proved difficult to resolve. The formerly enslaved resisted going back to work on the plantations even though compensated for their labor. Some rebelled and were dealt with quite severely. Others quit the plantations and were considered vagabonds who wandered the countryside posing a problem for security.

Agricultural production was on the rise but unable to reach the levels attained prior to 1789. Coffee became the main export while sugar production languished. Large plantations shrunk in size couldn't produce at the record levels achieved under the accursed slave system. Many grumbled at his harsh rule. Reluctant to trust, he kept his thoughts and plans to himself. As a ruler he was more feared than loved. He kept a tight leash on the local situation.

Toussaint's main threat came from France where another great leader emerged from the throes of the revolution. Napoleon Bonaparte, a brilliant general and astute politician, rose to become the sole master of France while Toussaint became the sole ruler of St. Domingue. France was finally at peace within and without. No longer at war with the other European powers and with law and order restored at home, Napoleon turned his attention to France's colonies. What he saw did not please him.

St. Domingue under Toussaint enjoyed more autonomy than France was willing to tolerate. The former planters wanted to return to St. Domingue to re-establish the slave system that had made them and the colony so rich. They pressured Napoleon, who was all too willing to go along with their desires. Napoleon, a virulent racist, was infuriated that a formerly enslaved man of African descent would govern France's most important profitable colony. St. Domingue's constitution was poorly received.

Napoleon prepared an army of invasion. It was time to teach Toussaint and those formerly enslaved a lesson. To that end, Napoleon entrusted one of his best generals and brother-in-law Charles-Victor Emmanuel Leclerc. This decorated general and trusted confidant was given the mission of defeating Toussaint, bringing St. Domingue back into line, and restoring slavery. He was equipped with a flotilla of ships and 20,000 top of the line soldiers, including veterans who had success in campaigns from Italy to Germany.

Leclerc's plan was to strike at several places and simply overwhelm Toussaint thus putting him on the defensive and preventing him from concentrating his forces. Toussaint, aware of the expedition sent against him, had a plan of his own that placed munitions in different parts of the interior to wage a guerilla campaign. General Christophe was ordered to burn Cap-Français to the ground, which he did. The cities were to be strategically evacuated and a retreat to the mountains would be the redoubt where the French armies would be bogged down. He planned for a long and drawn-out affair.

Toussaint's plan failed. After waging a war on several fronts his armies were defeated all along the coasts, and a good part of the interior was lost to the French. Toussaint's troops were decimated and their discipline broken. He was left with no viable path to victory. He elected to negotiate a surrender and was allowed a triumphant entry to Cap-Français to tender his official surrender. His guard of honor accompanied him. After a celebratory dinner, Toussaint left to go to his plantation in Ennery.

Toussaint sought a way back to power. But Leclerc's mission was to rid St. Domingue of its military leaders such as Dessalines and Christophe, and remove their soldiers from active service, demilitarize the colony and restore slavery. For the plan to succeed Toussaint had to be eliminated from the scene. He had been neutralized but one more step had to be taken.

While Leclerc had prevailed, there remained bands of Marrons who were devastating the countryside. They raided, then retreated to the mountains. Toussaint was rumored to be conspiring with the Marron leader Scylla. In fact, some letters that Toussaint wrote to Scylla were intercepted by the

French. Toussaint still had cards to play. What Leclerc feared most was that Toussaint could escape to the mountains and start a general insurrection. They had to remove Toussaint from the scene or else lose control.

Toussaint was invited to a meeting at a nearby plantation to consult with the local authorities. Normally suspicious, Toussaint chose to attend and was immediately seized, arrested and put on a ship to France. His family was arrested along with him. Toussaint predicted that by arresting him the French only chopped down the trunk of the tree of liberty. He accurately predicted that the roots were deep and numerous. These roots would sprout a new and stronger tree, thus ensuring the liberty of the formerly enslaved.

Once in France, Toussaint was transferred to Fort Joux a remote fort in the Jura mountains located near the Swiss border. There Toussaint spent the last days of his life. Most likely depressed, he was totally isolated. He asked to see his family, but all requests were denied. Toussaint died on the morning of April 7, 1803. He was found in his cell sitting beside the fire with his head slumped forward. One of the most remarkable men of any epoch died alone and filled with melancholy.

Toussaint was the father of our revolution. He belongs more to universal history than to our simple story. Toussaint's ambition propelled him into the world of geopolitics. He met with the English and Spanish, traded with the new American Republic and developed a foreign policy. The First Consul and then Emperor of France also had his geopolitical ambition and plans that ran counter to Toussaint's.

Each has left a legacy that resounds to this day.

For us, Toussaint is a figure on a pedestal, a hero who belongs to history. We hold him dear in our collective memory and shed tears when we retell the final chapter of his story. The cold and bitter isolation at Fort Joux, far from the tropical breezes and warm sun of St. Domingue. We reflexively shiver and grow silent at the thought of our hero's end. True to his name he was L'Ouverture, the way forward. The path that led to our independence. In our story, Toussaint is the prophet who paved the way for our salvation. He had to leave scene for the next chapter to unfold. [33] [34]

---

33. Saint-Rémy, Joseph, L'ouverture, Toussant "Mémoires du Général Toussant L'Ouverture par lui-même" Pagnerre, 1853

34. James, C.L.R *The Black Jacobins: Toussaint L'Ouverture and the San Domingo,*. London: Secker & Warburg (1938). Revised edition, New York: Vintage Books/Random House (1963).

6

THE FIGHT FOR FREEDOM

WITH TOUSSAINT physically removed from the scene, Leclerc showed his hand. The first step was to disarm the populace.[35] A number of armed groups resisted the order that Leclerc wanted to bring to St. Domingue. Many of the formerly enslaved, some of whom had served under Toussaint, vanished into the mountains and stockpiled their arms. What had Leclerc really won?

Toussaint's presumptive heir and nephew (Charles Belair) sought to rally all the armed bands under his banner and drive out the French, but was captured and executed. Then began a reign of terror to pacify the colony. Insurgents who

---

35. Bell, Madison Smartt (2008) [2007]. *Toussaint L'Ouverture: A Biography.* New York: Vintage Books.

were apprehended were summarily executed. This policy had the opposite effect from what Leclerc had anticipated. Indeed, the number of insurgents grew by the day.

Two digressions must be made: first is the presence of yellow fever in St. Domingue and the ravages it perpetrated on French troops. These troops unaccustomed to the tropical climate, succumbed in great numbers to this local fever. But the indigenous fighters did not fall prey to yellow fever.[36]

Some have suggested that yellow fever is one of the reasons why the French army was defeated by the army of independence. They argue that but for the decimation of the French troops by the fever, they would have prevailed. What goes unsaid is that similar French troops were sent to Martinique and Guadeloupe with the same mission, and yellow fever was present in those islands. Since the French prevailed there, clearly yellow fever was not sufficient to defeat them.

Taking this argument further, we might point to the Spaniards who defeated the Arawak and Taino on the island. Were these Spaniards immune to yellow fever? Many European armies successfully operated throughout their conquest of the Caribbean. It is laughable to pin the loss of St. Domingue on yellow fever.

––––––––––––––

36. ibid

In most wars the victor tells the story. In ours, the losers came up with their own fanciful reason for their military defeat at the hands of the army of independence.

The troops led by Dessalines and Christophe among the most celebrated generals were not a ragtag bunch. Trained by the French, they had fought many battles against Spanish and British troops to reclaim control of St. Domingue. In the salons of Europe where the mighty French army was both feared and respected it was easy to accept the excuse offered. Lest some Austrians, Spaniards, Germans, Italians, among others, who had been defeated by the mighty French would look foolish losing to an army that was defeated by an insurgent army of formerly enslaved and inferior Africans. Why was the formidable military of France able to control territories in the Caribbean and other regions with tropical climes with yellow fever and not conquer in St. Domingue? Facts are hard to ignore.

The other digression: the pointing to the acts of cruelty that insurgents were accused of committing. The planters who fled St. Domingue to France, Cuba, Louisiana and elsewhere spoke of the horrors at the hands of enraged and savage Africans caught up in a frenzy of violence that knew no bounds. Their stories, told and retold, took on a life of their own. The atrocities became more and more gruesome. This "fake news" was heard by those who had no context and predisposed to seeing the African as a lesser being.[37]

The propaganda of the planters hit a deep psychological cord with those disposed to believe. They asked themselves: could this happen here? What if it were to happen? Many policies were implemented and new restrictions imposed on the enslaved populations in the American South and other places where the planters feared similar retribution. Constant references were made to our revolution and the need to prevent something similar from happening.

Yes, there was violence and terror associated with our struggle for independence. We didn't initiate the violence. The terror and cruelty started with the slave system. We were snatched from our homes in the Gulf of Guinea, the Congo and other regions of Africa to be brutalized and treated as subhuman creatures who existed to serve a pampered and privileged minority of oppressors. Our terror responded to that which was first visited upon us. Our goal was never to oppress, enslave and dominate the planters, but rather to regain the freedom that had been stolen from us.

____

37. Dubois, Laurent (2012). *Haiti: The Aftershocks of History*. New York: Henry Holt and Company. p. 151.

We were not going to be given our freedom; the French planters and soldiers made that clear. We were alone with no one to help us. We were seemingly outmatched, and outgunned. We saw what happened in Martinique and Guadeloupe, and felt the terror coming. They wanted to enslave us again. Faced with that, we chose to fight. The blood flowed on both sides. We were not going to submit and, we would do whatever was necessary to prevail.

We have never apologized for what we did and how we secured our independence. Nor should we ever. We fought with a fervor that bordered on fanaticism. We had nothing to lose but our chains. We would be free.

Leclerc faced a problem in putting his plan into effect. The 20,000 soldiers and officers had rid St. Domingue of the British and Spanish invaders.[38] But what to do with this army now? If they summarily dismissed and dis-armed they could join the growing ranks of the insurgents. Yet they were needed to maintain order and to fend off other potential invasions by France's enemies. The soldiers that were brought from France saw their numbers reduced by yellow fever; they could not easily be replaced.

---

38. Dorsainvil, Dr. J. C. "Manuel Histoire D'Haiti" Editions Henri Deschamps; Portus Principis, 15 July 1934

The solution was to provide a certain degree of autonomy to the officers who led these troops and assign them to serve alongside the soldiers recently brought from France. The officers who led these armies were commissioned in the French armies and had distinguished themselves in battle. They had reached the rank of General in the French army and had to be treated with great caution. The names of these leaders brings a welcome ring to our ears: Jean-Jacques Dessalines, a brilliant tactician; Alexandre Pétion an able artillery officer, and Henri Christophe a fearless military hero. These men and the troops they led had remained loyal to France even after Toussaint was apprehended and set off to France.

All three were wary of the French and suspected Leclerc and his motives. They lived under the suspicious eyes of the colonial authorities who did not trust them. They witnessed the brutal suppression of Charles Belair and feared that they could be next. Eventually, they recognized that their positions were at best tenuous.

The dominoes began to fall when Pétion joined the insurgents and was quickly followed by Christophe and Dessalines. At that point, Leclerc and the French armies were no longer fighting insurgents who were poorly led and limited their battles to the remote parts of the colony. These battle-hardened leaders joined; now they forged a veritable army, one that would ultimately expel the French from our country. It can be said that in October 1802, the war for our independence truly began.[39]

Shortly thereafter, Leclerc died. He was embattled, depressed and simply tired. Yellow fever did the rest. His remains were returned to France and he was buried in the Pantheon along with the military legends of France. In his stead, General Donatien Rochambeau was chosen to lead the armies of France and the colony.[40] The inflexible Rochambeau turned out to be a poor choice. Despising the insurgents, he initiated a war of terror that had the opposite effect of what was intended. The ranks of the insurgents swelled and acts of vengeance were met in kind.

Rochambeau and the French believed that terror would win the day and that the cowed insurgents would realize the futility of resistance. They believed in their superiority over these formerly enslaved insurgents and felt they could break the will of the insurgents. The rebel army, now taking shape,

---

39. "Gazette Politique et Commecial D'Haïti" (PDF). P. Roux, petion de L'Empreur. November 22, 1802

40. Haynsworth IV, James Lafayette (2003). *The Early Career of Lieutenant General Donatien Rochambeau and The French Campaigns inthe Caribbean,* 1792–1794. Florida State University.

would not be intimidated. Rochambeau and the French army had met their match. The insurgents were fighting for their freedom and their lives. They knew that to be captured meant a slow and torturous death. They fought as if their lives depended on it.

The insurgents' most significant decision came when Pétion moved to unite under one supreme leader. Jean-Jacques Dessalines was chosen. By virtue of his rank, seniority, boundless energy and the fear that he inspired. He was a brilliant tactician who would rise to the challenge. Pétion was the first of the major insurgent leaders to rally to Dessalines' side. Mutual respect and admiration grew between these two leaders from different backgrounds.

That the Gens de Couleurs and the Noirs came together to fight under the banner of Dessalines shouldn't be taken for granted.[41] With hindsight it seems obvious that these two groups would form one force to defeat and drive out the French. But one must not forget the acrimonious civil war fought between these groups less than a decade before when Toussaint was challenged by the Mulâtre leader Andre Rigaud. The conflict, bloody and bitter, pitted two charismatic leaders. Rigaud's ambition and talent put him in Toussaint's crosshairs.

41. Lawless, Robert, and James A. Ferguson." *Encyclopedia Britannica*. February 7, 2018.

In the end Toussaint emerged victorious, and Rigaud left St. Domingue for France.

The pacification of St. Domingue by Toussaint left many hard feelings. One could even speculate as to whether the Mulâtres would have rallied to unite under Toussaint to expel the French. The fact that Pétion and his cohort rallied to Dessalines is one of the more important events on the way to our independence. This seminal event, speaks to the statesmanship and strategic vision of Dessalines and Pétion and their mutual commitment to defeat the French.

Pétion born free of a French father and Mulâtre mother, was sent to France and educated there. [42]Upon his return to St. Domingue he fought alongside Rigaud in the civil war against Toussaint. Dessalines[43] was born enslaved and rose in the ranks of the French army. He became Toussaint's most important lieutenant. He and Pétion realized that their interests were aligned and that the French would never recognize their freedom. This unified command would direct the war for the insurgents. Other notable leaders such as Christophe, Yayou, Romain and Capois fell into line.

---

42. Battier, Alcibiade Fleury; Rafina, Gesner (1881). "Sous les Bambous: Poésies" (in French). p. 209

43. Dorsaninvil, Dr. J. C. "Manuel Histoire D'Haiti" Editions Henri Deschamps; Portus Principis, 15 July 1934

As our rebellion broke out, geopolitical events turned against France. The tenuous truce that had prevailed in Europe began to fracture. France and England were again at war. English ships began to blockade the ports of St. Domingue. This left Rochambeau feeling isolated and exposed militarily. He decided to concentrate his troops in the cities and coastal areas, thus effectively abandoning the interior.

The one part of the colony that had yet to come to the side of the insurgents was the south. Long the stronghold of Rigaud and his lieutenants, it took General Nicolas Geffrard who had submitted to Dessalines' authority to get the south on board. His reputation as a disciplined and brave soldier convinced the leaders of the local bands to join under the unified leadership of Jean-Jacques Dessalines. The insurgency was united, and the interior of the country was ceded by the French. The stage was set.

The united insurgents led by Dessalines and Pétion met in Arcahaie in May 1803 to plan for the next phase of the war. At that reunion a flag was created for the soldiers to rally around. The French tri-color flag had the colors blue, white and red. The colors were seen as symbolizing the various groups in St. Domingue. The white for the Europeans, the red for the Mulâtres and the blue for the Africans. In a symbolic and powerful gesture, Dessalines ripped out the white, leaving the blue and red signifying the union of the Mulâtres and Noirs who would to forge our independence. The national motto *"l'union fait la force"* recognizes that the Mulâtres and Noirs shared a common interest in defeating the French and expelling them from our land.

The union that created Haiti was both symbolic and physical. United they could not be defeated. France hoped to divide and conquer. That the Mulâtres and Noirs could work together as one speaks to the greatness and foresight of our founding fathers. The oppressed united and overthrew their oppressors. It was an example for the world.

Jean-Jacques Dessalines was indefatigable always on horseback, and seemingly appearing where and when our army was most threatened. His steely resolve to fight without giving quarter inspired the armies wherever he appeared. His energy was inexhaustible, and he often put himself in harm's way to secure our victory.[44]

Another gallant and brave general was General Capois, leading his troops in battle in a final push to defeat the French. Capois needed his troops to take over a fortified

____

44. Wood, Marie V. "Dessalines: Emperor of Haiti." *Negro History Bulletin* 15, no. 2 (1951): 30–37. http://www.jstor.org/stable/44212499.

hilltop controlled by the French. Capois led the charge and was targeted by French snipers who shot at him and hit his hat that fell by the wayside. He continued to lead the charge. The next bullet struck his horse and felled the animal. Capois drew his sword and advanced. Rochambeau himself was defending this position. Moved by this act of valor, he ordered the firing stopped. With a loud beating of drums, Rochambeau's personal honor guard marched up to the insurgents to deliver this message: "General Rochambeau expresses his regard and admiration to the officer who has covered himself with such glory." Victory or death there was no other option.

By summer 1803, the tide was turning in our favor. The French were relegated to the coastal cities. The insurgents controlled the interior. The coastal cities of Jérémie and Jacmel were firmly in our control. Then began the siege of Port-au-Prince. The siege lasted a month and the French general surrendered. No longer a guerilla army, we had become a well-organized and modern army able to conduct siege warfare. About 15,000 troops were arrayed against the French in the siege of Port-au-Prince. Soon after Port-au-Prince was taken, les Cayes fell as well. The main coastal cities of the southern and western parts of the colony were in our control. Onto the north and Cap-Français.

Towards the end of 1803, the French had lost control of the west and south, including all the coastal cities.[45] French forces were reduced to the north with Cap-Français as their major stronghold. Dessalines set up his headquarters in Gonaives, preparing the final campaign to wrest control of the north and defeat the French once and for all. With an army of 27,000 troops and assisted by the fearless generals Christophe and Capois a plan was prepared. The French had heavily fortified Cap-Français making a long siege unappealing to Dessalines. He gambled on taking the offensive and launching an all-out assault.[46]

Vertierres was the last battle where Rochambeau himself faced off against Dessalines and was defeated. Rochambeau abandoned Cap-Français and turned himself over to the British as their prisoner. The indigenous army marched triumphantly into Cap Français. By December 1803 the French

---

45. Wood, Marie V. "Dessalines: Emperor of Haiti." *Negro History Bulletin* 15, no. 2 (1951): 30–37. http://www.jstor.org/stable/44212499.

46. Dorsainvil, Dr. J. C. "Manuel Histoire D'Haiti" Editions Henri Deschamps; Portus Principis, 15 July 1934

were thoroughly defeated and St. Domingue was free and independent. The war was over, and freedom secured.

This event continues to resonate as modern readers discover the enormity of this achievement and its impact on world history. Our race redeemed and the oppressor defeated. One must go back to Spartacus and the early days of the Roman Empire for an analogous attempt by slaves to free themselves. In the Roman instance, Spartacus was defeated, and slavery restored.[47]

What happened in St. Domingue in 1803 was forever etched into the minds of those who lived it and for those made aware. On the battlefields of St. Domingue, the myth of European racial superiority was shattered. For us who are descendants of those glorious ancestors, we are proud and grateful. The French were formidable and sought to hold onto their most prosperous colony. The war was fought on both military and psychological grounds. The French believed in their innate superiority and lost battle after battle.

Now all Europeans had to confront the fact that the Africans were not inferior. They were not going to be cowed by terror; they were not going to be outfoxed by superior military strategy. The will to win and the discipline on the field of

---

47. James, C.L.R *The Black Jacobins: Toussaint L'Ouverture and the San Domingo,*. London: Secker & Warburg (1938). Revised edition, New York: Vintage Books/Random House (1963).

battle belonged to the insurgents, not the French. We prevailed against the greatest odds. Ours is a singular event for which we take enormous pride.

Haitians are a proud people, and our pride comes from this achievement. Our rich and glorious history is shared by none other. Our gallant forefathers were not seeking a moral victory or symbolic point. They fought for total victory. The French did not negotiate an armistice, truce or other face-saving way out. They were defeated, and then ejected. David felled Goliath. The ogre was no more. For the rest of our history the European would not enslave Africans on the land that was renamed Haiti.

On January 1, 1804, in Gonaives, Haiti's independence was proclaimed.[48] The evening before, Dessalines convened his generals and other notables to hear the proclamation read before them. The scribe of the document was Chareron, among Dessalines' long serving and trusted secretaries. The document was full of legal and theoretical abstractions relating to freedom and liberty. The audience, unmoved, felt that it failed to capture the moment and mood.

After a long silence, Boisrond Tonnerre, full of passion, said the proclamation failed to capture the spirit and feeling of

____

48. Sutherland, Claudia (16 July 2007). "Haitian Revolution (1791-1804)". *Blackpast.org*

those who had fought to secure our independence. To paraphrase, he said that to write the constitution we need the skin of the whites as parchment, his cranium as inkwell, his blood as ink, and a bayonet as a pen. Dessalines stood up and ordered Boisrond Tonnerre to write the proclamation of our independence.[49] The new version better captured the emotions of those present.

The very next morning, the first day of the new year, generals, notables and people of all backgrounds were present to hear the fiery speeches that were given along with the proclamation of Haiti's independence. Those gathered swore to defend the independence of our country. Dessalines was proclaimed Governor-General. A new era had begun.[50]

---

49. Madiou, Thomas. *Histoire D'Haïti*. Port Au Prince: Imprimerie De JH Courtois, 1847

50. Dorsainvil, Dr. J. C. "Manuel Histoire D'Haiti" Editions Henri Deschamps; Portus Principis, 15 July 1934

7

MASSACRE

THE LONG, BLOODY AND BITTER war of independence left the victors with apprehension.

Many believed the French would return to reclaim their colony. That insecurity was reinforced by the fact that just years before Leclerc had landed with a large expeditionary force to subdue Toussaint's forces and allow the French to regain control of St. Domingue. Now, the victors planned to fortify the coastal cities and build forts to defend our hard-won freedom.

The French remaining in Haiti posed a problem for the new nation. There was a high degree of animosity toward the white population. Some proposed mass deportation, others called for an outright massacre.

The animosity towards the French ran deep. Hardly a person did not lose a loved one to the regime of terror imposed first by Leclerc and then Rochambeau. There was a strong desire for vengeance. Meanwhile, there was the fact that the assets of the former plantation owners could be seized. Many of the French who remained were unrepentant and vulgar in their attitudes toward the victors claiming that the French army would soon restore the former order. Lastly, the eastern part of the island was still under French control.[51]

Dessalines was aware of the thirst for vengeance.[52] He also knew that this was a potentially subversive population that could create problems for the new nation. These were not people who were willing to live and let live. At the end of January, 1804 in the first month of our independence Dessalines gave the order to massacre the white population of Haiti.[53] The

---

51. Dorsainvil, Dr. J. C. "Manuel Histoire D'Haiti" Editions Henri Deschamps; Portus Principis, 15 July 1934

52. James, C. L. R. (1989) [First published 1938]. *The Black Jacobins: Toussaint L'Ouverture and the San Domingo Revolution* (2nd ed.). New York: Vintage Books. pp. 373–374.

53. Philippe R. Girard (2005) *Caribbean Genocide: Racial War in Haiti, 1802–4,* Patterns of Prejudice, 39:2, 138–161

order was carried out throughout the country. All sort of horrors were visited upon the white population.

There is no way to justify the atrocities. The enemies of Haiti have long recounted the excesses and used it to further their propaganda, depicting us as bloodthirsty savages. It is a stain on our history. We can explain the motives without defending or justifying these actions. Premeditated, it presaged what has come to be known as "ethnic cleansing."

Exceptions were made. Generally, those deemed of value to the new nation were spared. Those included priests, teachers, tradesmen, doctors, pharmacists. These and some others were spared.[54] Our glorious achievement was marred by this dark episode.

---

54. Buck-Morss, Susan (2009). *Hegel, Haiti, and Universal History*. University of Pittsburgh Press. pp. 75

8

EMPIRE

I N MAY 1804 Napoleon Bonaparte was declared the emperor of the French. When the news of this event reached Haiti, certain individuals close to Dessalines convinced him that the title Governor General (the one once held by Toussaint) was not sufficiently prestigious for the leader of an independent nation. That September, Dessalines was proclaimed Emperor Jacques 1st of Haiti. An elaborate ceremony held in Cap-Haitien proclaimed to the world that Jean-Jacques Dessalines was to be known as Jacques the first emperor of Haiti.[55]

---

55. Wood, Marie V. "DESSALINES: EMPEROR OF HAITI." Negro History Bulletin 15, no. 2 (1951): 30–37.

Haiti was still culturally and socially a child of France. Events in France continued to have repercussions in Haiti. Elite Haitians continued to send their children to be educated in France. The intellectual and political life of France was followed by the literate segment of the Haitian population. That's an important context when giving thought to why Dessalines was proclaimed emperor. If it were good enough for Napoleon, then why not for Dessalines? Throughout our first century of existence, there was a focus and preoccupation on France and things French.

Dessalines' reign as emperor only lasted two tumultuous years. Slavery was abolished in Haiti. To kick start the economy a harsh regime of forced labor was instituted. Citizens in the rural parts of the country (the vast majority) were given a choice: join the military or till the fields. Dessalines was arbitrary, capricious and ruled through fear. What was effective for a general didn't work for an emperor. His reign of terror created resentment. Those closest to him conspired and ultimately assassinated him.

He was killed on the Pont Rouge on the way to Port-au-Prince in a macabre ambush. He was surrounded by his murderers who shot and felled him. His head was split open by a blow from a sabre and stabbed by a dagger.[56] His limbs, arms and fingers were cut from his torso. A crowd shouted, "death to the tyrant." His end was gruesome. His torso was left to decay until a humble woman named Marie-Sainte Dédé Bazile gathered and buried the remains.[57]

Dessalines' regime has not fared well in the memory of most Haitians. Yet he is the father of our country. Our first leader. Toussaint began the process and Dessalines was the author and architect of our independence. He remains the first among our ancestors whom we revere for securing our freedom. A brilliant general, who was ruthless and indefatigable in battle. The leader the insurgents needed to meet steel with steel, resolve with resolve. He fought unflinchingly and without mercy. He led and he brought victory. For these achievements, he is remembered. With the passage of time his achievements have surpassed his negatives as emperor. He was meant to lead men in victorious battle, and to secure our freedom and independence. He was not meant to govern. He is rightfully venerated. Without Dessalines, there would be no Haiti.

---

56. Corbet, Bob (October 1825) "A Brief History of Dessalines." American Missionary Register, VI (10), 292–297.

57. Braziel, Jana Evans (2005-10-05). "Remembering Défilée: Dédée Bazile as Revolutionary Lieu de Mémoire". Small Axe. 9 (2): 57–85.

Dessalines has lived on in his descendants three of whom became president of Haiti. He was the granduncle of Nissage Saget who ruled Haiti from 1870–74, the grandfather of Florvil Hyppolite who served as president from 1889–96 and the great-grandfather of Cincinnatus Leconte who was president from 1911–12. This is also part of the legacy that he left us.

9

KINGDOM

Dessalines' assassination led to a struggle for control. Christophe, initially elected President of the newly declared Republic of Haiti, came to Port-au-Prince to take control and was resisted by the generals from the west and south. Pétion led the opposition. Christophe laid siege to Port-au-Prince and was unsuccessful. He retreated to the North and set up a separate state. For the next 13 years Haiti was separated into two separate states with Christophe ruling in the north and Pétion in the west and south. Cap-Haitien was the capital of the north while Port-au-Prince remained the capital of the west and south. Christophe declared himself king and Pétion was elected president in the republic. We had an empire, kingdom and republic all within the first decade of our independence.[58]

Christophe was crowned Henri the first in a solemn ceremony in June 1811.[59] Along with his coronation he established a hereditary monarchy naming his son as his heir.[60] In turn, he found created a class of hereditary nobility made up by 4 princes, 8 dukes, 22 counts, 37 barons and 14 knights.[61] An able administrator with a passion for palaces and monuments, Christophe built several sumptuous palaces.[62] The most opulent and famous was Sans-Souci.[63] He even built a palace with 365 doors. His lasting achievement was the construction of the Citalelle Laferrière, a wonder of engineering and speaks to

58. Dorsainvil, Dr. J. C. "Manuel Histoire D'Haiti" Editions Henri Deschamps; Portus Principis, 15 July 1934

59. Monfried, Walter, "The Slave Who Became King: Henri Christophe," Negro Digest, Volume XII, Number 12, October, 1963

60. Cheesman, Clive (2007), *The Armorial of Haiti: Symbols of Nobility in the Reign of Henry Christophe,* London: The College of Arms,

61. Dorsainvil, Dr. J. C. "Manuel Histoire D'Haiti" Editions Henri Deschamps; Portus Principis, 15 July 1934

62. Griggs, E.L.; Prator, C.H., eds. (1968), *Henry Christophe and Thomas Clarkson: A Correspondence.*

63. Gauvin Alexander Bailey, *The Palace of Sans-Souci in Milot, Haiti (c. 1806–1813): The Untold Story of the Potsdam of the Rainforest* (Munich and Berlin, Deutscher Kunstverlag, 2017)

Christophe's ambitious vision. The Citadelle, a fortress built atop a mountain called Bonnet à l'Eveque, was meant to repel the invading French were they to return. This location provided the defenders with a view from on high as to the movements of any army that would invade the kingdom. It was to serve as the redoubt and point of resistance to any invasion.

The Citadelle is an historical monument that brings pride to all Haitians. It has been designated as a world heritage site. One of the few in the Western hemisphere. It took 20,000 individuals to build, and many lost their lives to fulfill Christophe's dream.[64]

To kickstart the economy Christophe chose to employ the corvée system of agriculture.[65] This amounted to forced labor, on the plantations, and was deeply resented by those forced back onto the plantations to produce. Those working on plantations were sent to work on the massive building projects such as the palaces and chateaux built by Roi Henri. The backbreaking work to construct the Citadelle left the populace at odds with its ruler, but Christophe's often despotic rule did result in an increased agri-

---

64. Dorsainvil, Dr. J. C. "Manuel Histoire D'Haiti" Editions Henri Deschamps; Portus Principis, 15 July 1934

65. "Henri Christophe, King of Haiti". King's College London Archives & Special Collections. King's College London. Archived from the original on 9 December 2021.

cultural production.

Christophe came to an agreement with the British not to threaten its Caribbean possessions in exchange for trade and warning of any impending attack by the French. Though unpopular, Christophe's kingdom was prosperous when compared to the Haitian republic to the south. His comprehensive legal system, known as the Code Henri[66], addressed civil as well as penal law. The notable progress in the kingdom, came at a cost that was too high for most of his subjects.

Christophe, autocratic and deeply unpopular, attempted on several occasions to invade the republic to the south only to be repelled. Many of his soldiers defected. Towards the end of his reign, he fell ill; some suspected a stroke. Now despondent, he feared that he would be assassinated (like Dessalines). Thus, he took his own life and was buried in a secret location in the Citadelle.

Roi Henri has left an indelible mark on the history of our nation. More feared than loved, he cut a dashing figure. One of the primary authors of our independence, he resides in the pantheon of our glorious ancestors along with Toussaint, Dessalines and Pétion. To capture a sense of the legacy that he left, family legend tells of people visiting the Dondon region

66. Code Henry; Cap-Henry; R.Roux, Imprimeur du Roi, 1812

of the north (where Christophe reigned) in the mid 20th century and speaking to peasants who put their hands to their foreheads and bowed to Roi Henri. More than a century after his death he was still remembered. Another part of his legacy is that the 17th President of Haiti Nord Alexis (1902–08) was the grandson of the first and only king of Haiti.

10

REPUBLIC

Alexandre Pétion was elected in March 1807 by the Senate, becoming the first president of the Republic of Haiti.[67] There was still the kingdom of Haiti to the north led by Christophe. In the eastern part of the island, control was unstable. The hold on power was tenuous. Several generals with a power base in the south believed they should rule. They were a constant threat to the republic's internal stability. In the north, Christophe not resigned to a divided country prepared several invasions of the territory of the republic.

In contrast with the absolute control and efficiency of the northern kingdom, the republic ruled by Pétion had lax

67. Pétion, Dantes. "President Alexandre Pétion." *Phylon* (1940–1956) 2, no. 3 (1941): 205–202.

controls. This manner of administration lasted for a half-century. Suiting both the times and the nation. There was no reign of terror nor a desire for absolute power. In contrast to the kingdom where large plantations formed the backbone of the economy. Pétion distributed land to those who had fought for our independence.[68] This set the stage for a redistribution of agricultural lands into small plots. The antithesis of the plantation economy.

For better or worse this feature of the Haitian economy has lasted to the present day. Peasants own and till their own small plots. They farm for subsistence and not toward export production. On a national level this causes the economy to function in a manner less profitable than the old system. On the other hand, those who were formerly enslaved were free and became owners of their own plots of land. These were tangible gains and were irreversible. The economies that Toussaint and Christophe presided over led to greater productivity at a cost. That cost was disproportionately borne by those who were formerly enslaved. They deeply resented having been tied to the plantation where they once were enslaved.

---

68. Dorsainvil, Dr. J. C. "Manuel Histoire D'Haiti" Editions Henri Deschamps; Portus Principis, 15 July 1934

One must acknowledge that nowhere else in the region did peasants own their land. The large land holdings of Latin America were a dominant feature of the agriculture sector of the independent republics across the Americas. In the U.S. after the abolition of slavery the formerly enslaved owned no land and became sharecroppers. The Haitian has a different story.

We fought for and sacrificed to gain independence. We kicked out the French. Society and economy were recalibrated. The old economic system was abolished. Average Haitians did gain something besides freedom from slavery, they gained economic freedom. It was the freedom to practice subsistence agriculture on a small plot of land that they owned. This was a pivotal transformation. From enslaved to landowner with the freedom to make individual economic decisions. Politics was handled far away in Port-au-Prince and was the pre-occupation of a small sector of the society. Haitian peasants were largely left to their own devices. Pétion's administration set into motion a structural pattern that explains why Haiti developed as it did. Our economy lagged, and peasants were not tied into the national economy as in other countries.

The Haitian revolution was true to its name. This wasn't a mere change of political leadership transforming a gentrified plantation owner from a servant of a distant king to a ruler of his fate. The economy and society didn't change after the so-called revolutions throughout Latin American and even in the United States. These wars of independence were fought so that the wealthy criollos no longer had to answer to Spain or for the principle of "no taxation without representation." In those places, after independence the lives of the peasants did not much change. In many cases slavery remained an important element to the socio-economic order. Peasants and enslaved did not enjoy the fruits of independence but rather toiled long hours on the same plantations for the same masters.

Only in Haiti was this different. Our peasants fought for something, and in return, obtained what was denied to their peers throughout the hemisphere. The Haitian had his freedom and his plot of land. Enslaved no more and free to cultivate his land. To make economic decisions of their choosing. Others who tell our story fail to recognize this achievement. We are proud and free in a way that others have yet to experience.

Another distinguishing feature of the Haitian experience is the definition as to who is considered Haitian. Automatic citizenship was granted to those of African descent or those of indigenous descent (meant to include the remnants of the original inhabitants of our land) the Arawaks. Thus, all of those of African or Amerindian descent who made it to our shores were automatically considered Haitian. Conversely, those of European descent were not to be automatically granted citizenship.[69] This created some measurable benefits for example, foreigners could not own land in Haiti. Imagine a place where a European cannot own land and does not have an automatic right to citizenship. A European would have less status under the law than the peasants of Haiti.[70]

Then there was the appeal to others of African descent to come to Haiti as a place of refuge. Those who could make it to our shores would be accepted and treated as citizens. Not many availed themselves of this option, but there were examples of migration of African-American communities to Haiti. In addition, there are many individual cases of Jamaicans and other residents of the nearby islands who made their refuge and enjoyed freedom in Haiti.

Thus, we have a novel concept of a state founded by the formerly enslaved reaching out to those in bondage and offering them asylum, freedom and citizenship. This speaks to the universality of the Haitian experiment. Not just for Haitians but meant to encompass all those of the African diaspora

---

69. Louis-Joseph Janvier, *Les Constitutions d'Haïti,* Paris, Marpon et Flammarion, 1886. Thomas Madiou, *Histoire d'Haïti,* Port-au-Prince, 1848, tome III, p. 489

70. Dorsainvil, Dr. J. C. "Manuel Histoire D'Haiti" Editions Henri Deschamps; Portus Principis, 15 July 1934

who had been enslaved. Add the Arawak in the concept of who would be a citizen. These ideas formed us in a way that is different. Our founding generation had a revolutionary vision, inspired by the French Revolution and the concept of the "natural rights of man." For those enslaved by an odious system, the shackles were broken, and a haven created for all those children of Africa.

11

PAN-AMERICANISM

IT STARTED with Francisco de Miranda, the Venezuelan revolutionary and military leader who stopped off in Jacmel on his way back to his native Venezuela. In a famous exchange with Dessalines, they discussed the best means of securing independence. After much back and forth, the impatient Dessalines uttered the famous phrase *"coupe tete brûler cayes"* (cut off heads and burn down houses).[71] This summed up Dessalines' approach. Miranda was warmly received by our Emperor and sent on his way with arms and men. It was the first demonstration of Haiti's support for the cause of liberty for Latin America.

71. Dorsainvil, Dr. J. C. "Manuel Histoire D'Haiti" Editions Henri Deschamps; Portus Principis, 15 July 1934

In 1815, when *el libertador* himself, Simon Bolivar was in exile he found his way to Haiti and landed in les Cayes.[72] Receiving a hero's welcome, he was brought to Port-au-Prince to meet with President Pétion. They got along famously and discussed politics, strategy and the struggle for Latin American independence. Bolivar found safety, support, munitions and men to continue with the struggle. Pétion imposed only one condition on the assistance provided: Bolivar must commit to free the slaves wherever he was victorious. True to his word, el Libertador, freed the slaves on his vast plantations. He was unable to convince the other revolutionaries to go along; some were enslavers who would not agree to go along. We Haitians have neither ignored nor forgotten that Bolivar was a man of honor whose commitment to freedom led him to do what others would not: declare freedom for all.

Bolivar again found himself in Jacmel to recuperate, recharge and plan his return. He again received arms and men to return to the struggle. Ultimately, he was able to liberate these countries from the yoke of the Spanish: Colombia, Venezuela, Ecuador, Peru and Bolivia. In some small sense Haiti contributed to the independence of the nations. Were it not for the

---

72. Marion, Alexandre Pétion, Ignace Despontreaux Marion, and Simón Bolívar (1849). *Expédition de Bolivar*

support and succor provided by the Haitian government under Pétion, events could have turned out differently. Who knows? Putting aside all speculation, Haiti can deservedly claim a role in creating the conditions that led to the Pan American independence movement. More important to the extent that slavery was abolished in the newly liberated Latin American republics forged by Bolivar, Haiti can claim some credit.

These events have largely gone unnoticed by those who have told our story. The first Inter-American conference held in Panama in 1826 did not include Haiti. In part due to pressure exerted by the United States under the influence of the powerful slavery lobby. The goal was to isolate Haiti. Even after having shown tangible support in the form of men, munition and money. Haiti was excluded.[73] Alexandre Pétion is not celebrated for his contribution to the cause of liberty for Latin America and most particularly for those who were enslaved.

The young nation was bereft of allies, friends or support. Unlike the nations of the post-colonial Third World who gained their independence without a long and bloody war of independence, Haiti had to struggle mightily just to survive.

---

73. Watson, Hilbourne. "Theorizing the Racialization of Global Politics and the Caribbean Experience." Alternatives: Global, Local, Political 26, no. 4 (2001): 449–83. http://www.jstor.org/stable/40645030.

We were surrounded by hostile neighbors who saw our nation as a threat to a particular way of life. Haiti's mere existence posed a threat to the slave system. Therefore, Haiti had to struggle to exist with no allies or support from other countries. Our best hope was to be left alone.

At the time that Pétion provided support to Bolivar, there was fear that the French could return with an armada to retake possession of its former colony. The northern kingdom under King Henri Christophe was busy building the stronghold of the Citadelle along with other forts to resist a potential invasion. Pétion courageously supported Bolivar though it meant creating tension with Spain that was still master of its Latin American colonies. We viewed our nation as a beacon for freedom especially for the enslaved. Pétion provided assistance with only one condition, free the enslaved.

Domestically, Pétion governed Haiti from 1807 until his death in 1818.[74] This was the first republic under the constitution of 1806. The Senate was responsible for electing the President. At that time Christophe was expected to be chosen but many senators feared that he would become too powerful and ultimately despotic. They chose Pétion. By temperament

---

74. Dorsainvil, Dr. J. C. "Manuel Histoire D'Haiti" Editions Henri Deschamps; Portus Principis, 15 July 1934

and policy, he was seen as a moderate. He faced early opposition in the Senate and in a showdown, he demonstrated a degree of unexpected resolve. The Senate was adjourned for a lack of a quorum for five years giving Pétion full reign over the government.

In addition to opposition from some senators, Pétion had to fight off Christophe's several attempts to take control of the country. The most menacing occurred in 1812 when Christophe laid siege to Port-au-Prince. In each instance Christophe was defeated. Ultimately, he ceased his attempts to defeat the republic.

There were a myriad of conspiracies and attempts to destabilize and to overthrow Pétion. The most important occurred in 1810 when General Rigaud who had fought against Toussaint returned to Haiti. Rigaud was one of the mulâtre leaders who remained popular in the south. Upon his return he conspired to take over and become president. This led to a schism wherein Rigaud was proclaimed president in the south. Pétion chose not to engage in a civil war and accepted this schism as a fait accompli. In return he negotiated an alliance so the two republics would be united against Christophe.[75]

---

75. ibid

This state of affairs, wherein Haiti had a kingdom and two republics lasted for two years until 1812 when Rigaud died. At that point the schism ended and General Jerome-Maximilien Borgella brought the south back into the unified republic. For the most part Haiti has remained a republic that has been governed by presidents with legislative and judicial branches. The strong executive has been the dominant form of governance. By and large the transfer of power has been violent. Few presidents have finished their original term of office.

This is why Pétion could last where the other founding fathers had little success in governing. He exercised power in a manner that could be called a velvet touch. There was never a period of terror or a clamp-down on the opposition to consolidate his hold on power. He governed with moderation and treated his opponents with leniency which was in marked contrast to the examples laid by Dessalines and Christophe.

The 1816 constitution[76] allowed the president to serve for life and the right to designate his successor. This strong executive was balanced by a senate responsible for electing the president or ratifying his chosen successor. In addition to the Senate where the members served nine year terms, there was lower chamber whose representatives served five year terms.

76. Louis-Joseph Janvier, *Les Constitutions d'Haïti*, Paris, Marpon et Flammarion, 1886.

The legislative branch was in session each year for three months from April-June. This constitution was in place until 1843 when some modifications were made. The main provisions of the constitution were used to govern the country until the 1860s. It was the longest lasting constitution in our history.

With the adoption of the constitution, Pétion no longer ruled by decree, or outside the bounds of a constitution. As the executive he had to govern alongside the legislative branch. The legislature went into session in 1817 leading to the usual political battles in a fully functioning constitutional republic.[77]

Pétion, now ill, no longer had the energy to fight the political battles. He no longer made his customary appearance at the military parades and was no longer seen in public. The end came March 29, 1818. He was widely mourned throughout the country. He was one of the very few Presidents to have lasted as long as he did and to die peacefully while in office. Upon his death the nation genuinely grieved. He was the last of the great authors of our independence after Dessalines and Christophe. The legacy that he left was far different from those other authors of our independence. Less famous or charismatic than his counterparts, he had a lasting impact on

---

77. Dr. François, Pétion, Alexandre "Fondation De La République D'Haïti Par Alexandre Pétion" 1944, L'auteur) Port-au-Prince

our history.

Pétion was not the military leader that either Dessalines or Christophe were. Still he ranked among our greatest military generals. As a political leader he proved to have a greater grasp of how to govern the country. He was patient where the others weren't. He chose to outlast his opponents. He did not resort to terror or violence to maintain public order or to stay in office. The land reform he initiated was unique and revolutionary. Land was given to those who had none. Haitian society was transformed from that point forward. The Haitian peasant had his land and freedom: fruits of the long struggle for independence.

Under Pétion, Haiti tirelessly sought to end slavery in the hemisphere. Our support for Miranda and Bolivar provided eloquent testimony. Haiti stood as a beacon to those enslaved throughout the hemisphere and opened its arms to the enslaved who could make it to our shores. That is the legacy left by Pétion, who has been overlooked by many when they recount our history. He deserves to be remembered with respect and affection.

12

STABILITY

Jean-Pierre Boyer was widely recognized as Pétion's successor. He was his private secretary and closest political
collaborator. Upon Pétion's death it was left to the Senate
to select the next President. General Borgella was popular
among many of the senators, but in the end, Boyer was chosen.
Elected President for life, he ruled the Haiti for 25 years.[78] For
21 of those 25 he ruled over the entire island. The longest
serving President in the history of the country he brought
peace to the republic.

Boyer was born in Port-au-Prince in February 1776. His
father was a French tailor, and his mother from the Congo.

---

78. Baur, John Edward. "Mulatto Machiavelli, Jean Pierre Boyer, and The Haiti of His
Day." *The Journal of Negro History* 32, no. 3 (1947): 307–53.

Educated in France, he fought as a battalion commander during the French Revolution. He was allied with Andre Rigaud and fought against Toussaint in the bloody civil war won by Toussaint. Boyer and Pétion were among the officers who went back to France in exile. He returned to St. Domingue as part of the expeditionary army led by Leclerc to wrest control of the colony from Toussaint.

When it became clear that the French intended to restore slavery, Boyer and Pétion joined the indigenous army under Dessalines. When Pétion became president Boyer benefited because of their close relationship. He was one of the closest political collaborators that Pétion had. Boyer was the head of the Presidential guard a very powerful and prestigious position at that time.

The republic inherited by the second president of Haiti was threatened in the north by the kingdom of Henri Christophe and by a rebellion led by Goman in the territory of the republic. Goman, a Marron leader during the war of independence, controlled part of southwestern Haiti. He was financed in part by Christophe as a means of destabilizing the republic. He remained the supreme leader of his group of Marrons and governed his territory in full defiance of Port-au-Prince.

After Pétion's death, Boyer dispatched six regiments to put an end to the insurrection and take back control of the area under Goman's control. Led by Generals Bazelais and Borgella, the insurrection was put down and the territory reclaimed. In one year, Boyer had achieved something that his predecessor had not. Goman's insurrection had lasted from 1807–19. As of 1819 the Republic was in total control of the south and west departments of Haiti, leaving the north under the rule of Christophe.

In 1820, Christophe was felled by a stroke. His health was failing. His rule was unpopular, and his weakness led to conspiracies and ultimately to a revolt. His soldiers abandoned him, and Christophe did not want to be killed or taken alive so he killed himself with a silver bullet. His remains are buried in a secret location in the Citadelle, the fortress that he built.[79]

Boyer seized the moment. He mobilized the army and marched north. The local population acclaimed him and as he entered Cap-Haitien was greeted with cheers. The crowds chanted, "long live the president of Haiti." The uniting of the country was achieved without firing a single shot. After

---

79. Dorsainvil, Dr. J. C. "Manuel Histoire D'Haiti" Editions Henri Deschamps; Portus Principis, 15 July 1934

one year in office, Boyer had pacified the south by defeating Goman and then took control of the faltering kingdom of Haiti upon Christophe's demise. Never again would Haiti be divided into competing states. Nor would there be a long-lasting insurrection whereby a portion of the territory was not under the control of the government. For the first time since 1807 the country was united.

In the end what best suited our country was the velvet touch and the rule of law under a constitutional republic. Power in the hands of one ruler was established. There would be one person at the helm. The reason that Pétion won out over the others was the recognition that he did not have to rule by terror. Pétion lasted because he and those surrounding him understood that one could rule without recourse to violence, terror and fear.[80]

Boyer applied that lesson with great success. The north was tired of the repression of Christophe, and the populace was happy to be rid of him. Within a year and without the loss of a single life, Boyer unified the country. From that moment forward, Haiti has been governed by a powerful executive. The vision as to how to rule the country was accepted. This was an important step.

---

80. ibid

13

SANTO DOMINGO

IN DECEMBER 1821 there was a revolt in Santo Domingo against the Spanish.[81] The eastern two-thirds of the island of Hispaniola belonged to Spain and maintained as a colony that had long lost its place of prominence amongst Spain's New World possessions. After the conquest of the Aztecs and Incas had opened the doors to Central and South America, the colony of Santo Domingo became an afterthought. Just prior to the dawn of the French Revolution the population numbered approximately 125,000 which 50,000 were European, 60,000 mixed race and 15,000 enslaved Africans.[82]

---

81. Dorsainvil, Dr. J. C. "Manuel Histoire D'Haiti" Editions Henri Deschamps; Portus Principis, 15 July 1934

82. Hazard, Samuel, *Santo Domingo: Past and Present, with a Glance at Hayti,* Harper & Brothers, 1873

Santo Domingo, the capital, boasted the oldest church and university in the Americas. This sparsely populated colony became a pawn of the European powers during the French Revolution. In 1801, Toussaint invaded the East and united the island under the banner of the French Republic. Napoleonic France continued to control the colony after the declaration of Haiti's independence. When the European allies had finally defeated Napoleon, Santo Domingo reverted back to Spain in 1814. The local population rebelled against Spain in 1821.

With Spain defeated, the rebels were divided. Some merely wanted reforms in the way Spain governed its colony. Others wanted independence pure and simple. Yet another faction wanted to unite with Gran Colombia and form part of the Bolivarian compact. The most influential group wanted to unite the island under the Haitian banner.[83]

Boyer seizing the moment, as he had done a year earlier after the death of Christophe, massed an army of 20,000 soldiers at the border and proceeded to unite the island. The Haitian army met with little resistance. Boyer at the head of his army reached Santo Domingo in February 1822. For the first time

---

83. Dorsainvil, Dr. J. C. "Manuel Histoire D'Haiti" Editions Henri Deschamps; Portus Principis, 15 July 1934

since Columbus landed in 1492, the island was united and free from Spain and the control of the European powers.[84]

For the next 22 years, the island of Hispaniola was ruled by Haiti. Given the volatile political history of both countries, that there was political stability spanning two decades is quite an achievement. In fact, for the rest of the century neither country would experience such a long and stable period.

The Haitian occupation has been widely criticized from the Dominican point of view.[85] Indeed, the departure of Haiti from the eastern side of the island is commemorated as the Dominican Republic's day of independence. Notwithstanding that after having expelled Haitian rule, Spain returned and restored the colony of Santo Domingo. Even though the Dominicans later on expelled the Spanish, their liberation from Haiti is when they celebrate their independence.

From the Haitian point of view there aren't a great deal of mea culpas or handwringing over the occupation. The main benefit of the occupation was to unify the island thus, negating the possibility of invasion from the east. Moreover, control over the east by a European power would constitute a threat to

84. Baur, John Edward. "Mulatto Machiavelli, Jean Pierre Boyer, and The Haiti of His Day." *The Journal of Negro History* 32, no. 3 (1947): 307–53.

85. Martínez, Samuel. "Not a Cockfight: Rethinking Haitian-Dominican Relations." *Latin American Perspectives* 30, no. 3 (2003): 80–101. http://www.jstor.org/stable/3185037.

Haitian independence. From the Haitian perspective this had to be addressed. The other benefit of the Haitian occupation was the emancipation of the enslaved.

It is interesting to note that certain historians write about the emancipation of the enslaved Dominicans without celebrating that event. The enslaved were not a large part of the population as was the case in St. Domingue. In fact, the largest part of the population was those of mixed heritage. The historians who write this part of Dominican history are not taking the point of view of those formerly enslaved. It took the Haitians to bring them their freedom. Who knows how long it would have taken for the Dominicans themselves to free the enslaved? True to the spirit of fraternity, the Haitians freed themselves, and in turn freed the enslaved in another land. This is an overlooked achievement of the Haitian nation.[86]

The Haitian occupation operated to the benefit of Haiti to the detriment of the Dominicans. In fact, it reinforced the sense of difference between the two peoples. The occupation was a defining moment in the sense of nationhood for the Dominicans. The language, customs, economy and social

---

86. Dorsainvil, Dr. J. C. "Manuel Histoire D'Haiti" Editions Henri Deschamps; Portus Principis, 15 July 1934

structure were different from Haiti. The Haitian government was unable to provide food, supplies and shelter for the troops sent to occupy the east. Consequently, the army requisitioned food and supplies at gunpoint from the local population.

The Haitian constitution forbade white ownership of land. Thus, many leading landowners fled the country for Cuba. This led to an exodus. Lastly, burdensome taxes were levied on the Dominicans to help repay the indemnity that Haiti agreed to pay France for its independence. The Dominican economy was transformed to provide agriculture for exports whereas ranching had been an important feature of the Dominican economy.

The occupation was most resented in the capital of Santo Domingo and by the elites whose control was diminished. The island was "one and indivisible" to quote Boyer and remained thus for 22 years.[87] The colonial experience of the two peoples were quite different. Santo Domingo wasn't the richest colony in the Spanish colonial empire. Vast fortunes were not made on the backs of the enslaved. As was discussed the enslaved population was a minority whereas in St Domingue the enslaved made up the vast majority.

---

87. "Dominican Republic –Haiti and Santo Domingo". *Country Studies*. Library of Congress; Federal Research Division.

Haitians therefore brought their experience and history with them and projected and imposed our culture on a population ill-suited for the experiment. Haiti's occupation failed on many levels and the Haitians themselves didn't do well as colonial masters. But it's worth noting that the average Dominican was treated no better and notably no worse than the average Haitian.

The occupation failed but was inspired for valid strategic reasons. Interest in having the eastern part of the island out of the hands of the European powers continued to preoccupy many a Haitian government after the Dominicans had secured their independence.

14

INDEMNITY

To HAVE OUR INDEPENDENCE recognized by one of the major powers, we concluded a treaty with France thereby securing France's recognition of Haiti's independence. Consequently, other nations could follow and recognize our independence. For those governing Haiti at the time, the recognition of our independence by France was imperative.[88] That single act would remove the threat of any future invasions.[89] It had to be secured at all costs.

The most onerous provision of the treaty caused France to receive an indemnity of 150 million francs. This indemnity

---

88. Leger, J.N. *Haiti: Her History and Her Detractors.* The Neale Publishing Co.: New York & Washington. 1907.

89. Leyburn, James (1961). *The Haitian People.* Yale University Press.

was to pay the property claims the French lost as a result of the Haitian revolution.[90] In exchange for diplomatic recognition, Haiti had to pay with its treasure. Imagine! A sovereign nation paid for its independence after a successful military expulsion of their former masters. Contrast this with the post-colonial period independence in the 20th century, where new nations were granted independence along with economic assistance.

Haitians are indeed unique in this. We paid for our independence twice; once on the battlefield in 1804 and at the table of diplomacy in 1825. Our freedom was won at an exorbitant price. The motivation for agreeing to this onerous indemnity was the political and diplomatic isolation faced by the new nation, and the constant threat of a French invasion.

Prior to the treaty, France did not completely surrender its efforts to reclaim Haiti. St. Domingue had been its richest colony, and there was an active political camp that wanted to take it back. The post-Napoleonic king of France Louis XIII sent several missions beginning in 1814, then again in 1816 and even in 1822. Each emissary sought to restore Haiti to

---

90. Gamio, Lazaro; Méheut, Constant; Porter, Catherine; Gebrekidan, Selam; McCann, Allison; Apuzzo, Matt (2022-05-20). "Haiti's Lost Billions". *The New York Times.*

France.[91] But they were told that Haitians would fight with all of their might to maintain our independence.

Pétion had discussions with the emissaries and offered to pay an indemnity of a modest sum to France in exchange for diplomatic recognition. In 1824, a French mission was accompanied by a naval armada prepared to invade.

Haiti was isolated diplomatically. The United States whose, southern planters feared a Haitian style revolution marginalized and further isolated Haiti. Great Britain who might have been expected to recognize Haiti's independence as a counterweight to French influence in the Caribbean also failed to recognize our independence. The British recognized the newly created Latin American republics but not Haiti. Latin American republics excluded Haiti from the Pan American Conference of 1826.[92]

The threat of invasion was real, and Haitian governments had to arm and prepare to repulse a potential invasion.[93] Along with the political in-fighting and instability that marked the

---

91. Dorsainvil, Dr. J. C. "Manuel Histoire D'Haiti" Editions Henri Deschamps; Portus Principis, 15 July 1934

92. Watson, Hilbourne. "Theorizing the Racialization of Global Politics and the Caribbean Experience." *Alternatives: Global, Local, Political* 26, no. 4 (2001): 449–83. http://www.jstor.org/stable/40645030.

93. Leger, J.N. *Haiti: Her History and Her Detractors.* The Neale Publishing Co.: New York & Washington. 1907.

first decades of our independence, the nation was required to maintain a war footing. This wreaked havoc on the budget creating a role for the military that left the generals as all powerful in the political sphere.

The lack of diplomatic recognition impinged on the ability to arrange for trade with neighbors on terms that could be considered reciprocal. Consequently, Haiti's trade arrangements with the rest of the world were precarious. Access to new markets or incentives for others to increase trade with us did not exist. The importation of arms and munitions and the maintenance of a large standing army was also deleterious to the young nation. In short, Haiti was in a vise and choking. France applied pressure and an agreement was struck.

Much criticism has been generated about the wisdom of the indemnity. Those leading the country at the time believed it the best course of action. With the passage of time, the consequences of the indemnity came to define how it was viewed. The stress placed on the economy to pay down the 150 million Francs was significant. The amount was reduced to 90 million in 1838. It took until 1893 for the last indemnity payment to be paid to France. Up until that time the debt was managed by taking out loans at usurious rates of interest from foreign banks.[94] The interest payments alone were difficult to manage given the country's meager resources.

Because of the indemnity, the economy had to be oriented toward earning foreign currency in order to service the debt. Moreover, the money needed precluded investments in infrastructure, education or other nation building measures. The burden placed on Haiti was heavier than that faced by other nations. We acknowledge what others do not. Our circumstances were so unique that rather than point to the shortcomings of our development it is a massive achievement to have paid for our independence in blood and treasure.

How unfair it was to the young nation to have been forced to repay the very people that had been our oppressors. No other people have been forced to endure the most wretched form of enslavement, then fight a prolonged and bloody war for independence only to then have to repay its oppressors. Haiti paid an extraordinary price for its independence.

---

94. Gamio, Lazaro; Méheut, Constant; Porter, Catherine; Gebrekidan, Selam; McCann, Allison; Apuzzo, Matt (2022-05-20). "Haiti's Lost Billions". *The New York Times.*

15

END OF AN ERA

DURING THE PERIOD of time that Boyer ruled Haiti, there was a program of emigration of African Americans to Haiti. In 1824, there were 6,000 immigrants who came to Haiti to enjoy freedom and to lead lives as citizens of the world's only Black Republic.[95] Free people of color left New York, Philadelphia and Baltimore to settle in Haiti. Our nation served as a beacon of freedom to all the enslaved and in North America there was a keen interest in the new republic. Of those who went to Haiti, many came back disillusioned. There was a failure to adapt to the local culture, language and customs. Some found that there was no support offered by

---

95. Dorsainvil, Dr. J. C. "Manuel Histoire D'Haiti" Editions Henri Deschamps; Portus Principis, 15 July 1934

the government in their relocation to a new country. For those who remained the promise of freedom in a Black republic held true. They and their descendants remained in the region of Samana (currently in the Dominican Republic).

Under Boyer, Haiti was the first government to recognize the Greek revolution against the Ottoman Empire. Boyer sent a letter to the Greek expatriates living in France offering the moral support of the Haitian nation. As a poor country whose resources were limited, Boyer articulated his political and moral support.[96] Some historians claim that Boyer sent 25 tons of Haitian coffee to Greeks to be sold to finance the revolution. Others claim that 100 soldiers were sent as well. None of these claims have been verified but nonetheless can speak to the role that the young nation played on the world stage. Just as with Bolivar and Pétion, Boyer stood with those fighting for their freedom from oppression.

In May 1842 an earthquake struck the entire island and brought devastation to Port-au-Prince, Cap-Haitien and to the east Santo Domingo and Santiago.[97] The economy

---

96. Sideris, E.G., and A. A. Konsta. "A Letter from Jean-Pierre Boyer to Greek Revolutionaries." *Journal of Haitian Studies* 11, no. 1 (2005): 167–71. http://www.jstor.org/stable/41715298.

97. Bakun W.H. & Flores C.H. (2011). "Historical Perspective on Seismic Hazard oo Hispaniola and the Northeast Caribbean Region" (PDF). *Journal of Geophysical Research*. American Geophysical Union.

worsened. Boyer's opponents used that devastation and the government's weak response to justify insurrection. With the economy worsening and with the desire for change, the insurgents prevailed. Boyer's government adopted policies of austerity. These measures led to general discontent across the island and the earthquake tipped the balance against the government.

A generation of younger individuals wanted change. They were not of the revolutionary generation and resented the lack of opportunities for advancement. After 25 years in power, Boyer and his government had run out of steam. Led by General Charles Rivière-Herrard, the revolt succeeded.

In February 1843 Boyer left Haiti for Jamaica. He was the first of many overthrown presidents who left for Jamaica. Boyer settled in France and lived in Paris. He was presented at court to the then King of France, Louis-Phillippe. The king wanted to honor Boyer by referring to him as prince. Boyer, ever the Republican, insisted that he was no prince and that he was only the ruler of a small republic. To which the king replied anyone who has ruled over 1 million people over a quarter century deserves to be called a prince.[98]

---

98. Baur, John Edward. "Mulatto Machiavelli, Jean Pierre Boyer, and The Haiti of His Day." *The Journal of Negro History* 32, no. 3 (1947):

Boyer died destitute in 1850, in Paris, the first of many Haitian presidents to taste the bitter death of exile in a foreign land in a state of penury. This second president of Haiti like many others who followed was not corrupt. They did not control the coffers of the republic as if it were their personal bank account. Many were scrupulous about keeping their finances separate from those of the state. This reality runs counter to the general description by others of our first-century presidents as being corrupt dictators.

Boyer was neither corrupt nor a dictator. In the years that Boyer ruled there was neither political violence nor repression. Political opponents were not killed. Neutralized maybe, but not through violence. Was the implicit threat of violence used to cower the opposition? Most likely.[99]

Boyer, perhaps unpopular toward the end of his rule, was alone among the presidents of both Haiti and Dominican in the 19th century who provided two decades of peace and stability. In fact, the threat of invasion from France was eliminated (albeit at an astronomical price). The island was united under one government. A haven for freed people of color was established. Haiti was a supporter of the struggle for liberation in the case of Greek independence. When contrasted with his

---

99. ibid

predecessors and with those who followed this was a consequential and unmatched record of governance.

Boyer's need to assure the independence of Haiti by signing a treaty with France can be called the second act in the independence drama. Yet this came at the price of any potential prosperity for the young nation. The economy was structured to generate revenues to pay off the debt that was contracted. Haiti was in a sense condemned never to experience the wealth that had defined St. Domingue. In the context of our history, Boyer must be considered among the greatest presidents.

After Boyer the period of the revolution was over. The generation of generals who secured our independence were aging. A new generation was ready to take over. Before we discuss how this next generation impacted our history, we need to complete our story by telling the stories of the women who also fought in our glorious struggle for freedom and independence.

16

HEROINES OF THE REVOLUTION

As happens so often, however unfairly, the men have received the accolades and were out front in the fight for our freedom. The Haitian revolution knew no bounds of decency. The women, children and other vulnerable populations weren't spared. They had to endure privations, misery, sacrifice and gave us countless examples of heroism. Here are but a few of those women who have been widely recognized for their contributions.

The first woman of note has not been named. She was the priestess who conducted the ceremony in the Bois Cayman that led to the insurrection in the plaine du Nord in 1791. We have been told that she danced, swayed and sang. She pirouetted and all eyes were transfixed on her that night. Like the unknown soldier, her name is not known to us, but the role she played is well known. She and Boukman were there at the beginning. She led and inspired those gathered to follow through and lit the fire that engulfed St. Domingue. That flame has yet to be extinguished and lives in the hearts of every Haitian. Some believe that she was Cécile Fatiman[100] who was a renowned priestess.

Sanite Belair,[101] served with Toussaint's army along with her husband (Charles Belair). She became a sergeant and rose to the rank of lieutenant. She and her husband were taken prisoner and sentenced to death. Her bravery in the face of execution gives her a special place in the annals of our war for independence.

Catherine Flon,[102] best known as the seamstress who at the request of Dessalines sewed our first flag. She nursed our sick and wounded soldiers during the war of independence.

---

100. Joan Dayan, *Haiti, History, and the Gods*, University of California Press, 1998

101. James, C.L.R. (1963). *The Black Jacobins; Toussaint L'Ouverture and the San Domingo Revolution* (2d ed., rev ed.). New York: Vintage Books. p. 252

102. Méléance, Elmide. (2006) "Catherine Flon and the Creation of the Haitian Flag," in *Revolutionary Freedoms: A History of Survival, Strength*. Coconut Creek, FL, Caribbean Studies Press

Marie-Jeanne Lamartinière,[103] a soldier who fought in the decisive battle of Crete-a-Pierrot. In the uniform of a male soldier, she is remembered for her courage and skills as a strategist as well as rifle and sword. When not fighting, she nursed the injured and wounded. Victoria "Toya" Montou, fought in Dessalines' army and was reputed to have been a warrior in the Dahomey Empire before being enslaved. She escaped the plantation and became a fierce soldier.

Marie Sanité Dédée Bazile recovered the remains of Emperor Jean-Jacques Dessalines after his assassination.[104]

Suzanne Simone Baptiste L'Ouverture,[105] the wife of Toussaint was imprisoned taken prisoner by Napoleon's forces after the capture of her husband. She suffered horrific torture to reveal the whereabouts of Toussaint's treasure, but never did.

Marie-Claire Heureuse Felicité [106] the first Empress of Haiti as the wife of a Jacques the 1st. An educator, she taught French to the once enslaved.

---

103. Madiou, Thomas (1803). *Histoire d'Haïti: 1799–1803* (in French). Editions H. Deschamps.

104. Braziel, Jana Evans (2005-10-05). "Remembering Défilée: Dédée Bazile as Revolutionary Lieu de Mémoire". *Small Axe.* 9 (2): 57–85.

105. James, C.L.R. (1963). *The Black Jacobins; Toussaint L'Ouverture and the San Domingo Revolution* (2d ed., rev ed.). New York: Vintage Books. p. 252

106. Manigat, Mirlande (2002). *Etre Femme en Haiti Hier et Aujourd'hui*. Port-au-Prince, Haiti: Université Quisqueya. p. 336

Marie-Louise Coidavid,[107] the first and only queen of Haiti. Married to King Henri. Ended her life in exile in Italy.

Marie-Madelaine Lachenais (Joute),[108] the mistress and political advisor to Presidents Pétion and Boyer. She was the de facto First Lady of Haiti. She exerted considerable political influence over the republican period of Haiti's early history. She bore two daughters with Pétion and one with Boyer. Arguably, the single most powerful woman in the history of Haiti, died in exile in Jamaica.

These women highlighted are the most well-known of the many who played an important role in the independence of Haiti. They fought alongside the male soldiers, suffered the same fate as the men in battle, and upon capture were tortured, mistreated and executed. Women played a crucial role in our independence from priestesses, nurses to warriors. our story is not complete without singing their praises.

---

107. Louis Marceau, *Marie-Louise d'Haiti*, Publié à Buenos Aires, Se, 1953

108. Placide David, *Cité Dans Femmes Haïtiennes*, op.cit. p67

17

INSTABILITY

THE GOVERNMENTS that followed Boyer were unable to maintain the stability that the country had known for decades. There was considerable infighting among those who would replace Boyer. The drafting of a new constitution exposed many of those fissures. Rivalries were based on personal rather than policy differences as prominent generals vied to take power into their hands. Rivière-Hérard was the first of those who ruled Haiti after Boyer. He was president from December of 1843 to May of 1844.[109]

The eastern part of the island took advantage of the instability generated by the change in government and rebelled.

---

109. Dorsainvil, Dr. J. C. "Manuel Histoire D'Haiti" Editions Henri Deschamps; Portus Principis, 15 July 1934

The population was much aggrieved by restrictive measures taken to repay the indemnity. There was a fundamental difference in the approach to the way the Catholic Church was treated by the Haitian government. Among the biases of the French Revolution that took hold in Haiti was a secular approach to the Catholic Church that was not shared by the eastern population.

The Church had a different historical experience in the east and the population had a different relationship with the Catholic Church. Many Dominicans were appalled by the treatment of the Church on behalf of the secularist republican diehards who governed Haiti. This led to the chants of "Vive la Vièrge Marie" in the eastern part of the island. The attachment to religion was a factor in the development of a nascent sense of nationhood in the east.

Rivière-Hérard led a force of 25,000 men to regain control of the rebellion in the east.[110] While he was away there was considerable political intrigue back in Port-au-Prince. Those who had supported Boyer used his absence to overthrow the government. They settled on another general to replace

---

110. Calhoun, John Caldwell; Wilson, Clyde Norman (1959). *The Papers of John C. Calhoun*, Volume 21. Univ of South Carolina Press.

Rivière-Hérard as president. Philippe Guerrier was persuaded to take over in May 1844. Rivière-Hérard took the path of many deposed presidents of Haiti, and went into exile in Jamaica.

A key factor leading to the overthrow of the Rivière-Hérard was the popular insurrection in the south led by peasants using pikes as weapons. Becoming known as the "piquets," they were to exercise considerable influence in the years to come. Led by Jean-Jacques Açaau, this band of fighters defeated a portion of the army and took the southern city of Les Cayes. The momentum from this victory led to a march on Port-au-Prince.

The political vacuum left by Boyer's departure led to a political tinderbox where all the factions that had been manipulated and neutralized by Boyer came to the fore. The southern peasants wanted to vent their frustrations and anger because of difficult economic conditions. Moreover, they resented those who were enriching themselves in the cities while the peasants were languishing. They marched on Port-au-Prince instilling fear and apprehension on the part of the residents of the capital. The piquets were defeated by the army at Miragoane and the threat was contained. Philippe Guerrier became the fourth president of Haiti in May 1844, the third within a year.[111]

Guerrier, an octogenarian born in 1757, lasted only a year in office before dying. He is among the few presidents who passed away while still in office (Pétion was the first). He was old and feeble and manipulated by those who put him in office. These individuals were included in the twenty-one member Conseil d'État. Septimus Rameau, the real power behind the throne was arbitrary and dictatorial. He governed by force and toward the end signed orders to arrest and detain his opponents.

Upon Guerrier's demise the Conseil d'État (Council of State) settled upon another octogenarian general and veteran of the war of Independence. Louis Pierrot[112] was from the north and a brother-in-law to Henri Christophe. This was another case of putting on the "throne" a revered general from the past who would be easily manipulated by the Council of State. Pierrot, born in 1761 became president at the age of 84, and was widely reputed to suffer from dementia. He abhorred living in Port-au-Prince and perceived

---

111. Bellegarde-Smith, Patrick. "Haitian Social Thought in the Nineteenth Century: Class Formation and Westernization." Caribbean Studies 20, no. 1 (1980): 5–33. http://www.jstor.org/stable/25612884.

112. Léger, Jacques Nicolas (1907). *Haiti: Her History and Her Detractors*. The Neale Publishing Company.

assassins everywhere.

One day he decided to leave Port-au-Prince without notifying anyone. When his absence was discovered there began a mad search for him. On his way to his favorite residence in Camp Louise, he could not be persuaded to return to Port-au-Prince. Thus in 1845 the capital of the country was moved to Cap-Haitien. All government functions and officials had to move to the new capital. Few favored this move making the government more unpopular by the day.

Pierrot was also fixated on the eastern part of the island. Like others of his generation, he was not reconciled to the independence of the Dominican Republic. One of the first acts of his government was to issue a proclamation calling for the union of the island. The Dominicans took the offensive by seizing the frontier towns of Hinche and Las Cahobas. This offensive was repulsed, and the Dominicans were sent back across the border. This led to a stalemate and localized skirmishes in the border region. Unsatisfied, Pierrot wanted a new campaign to unify the island but there was little enthusiasm for a war with the Dominican Republic.

By 1846 the discontent was widespread. In the city of St. Marc troops were being mustered to march on the Dominican border. Instead, they mutinied, marched on Port-au-Prince and clamored for General Jean-Baptiste Riche as the new president.[113]

Born in 1780, Riche served in the army under Henri Christophe rising to the rank of general and deputy commander. He was among Christophe's most trusted commanders. Placed in command of the north, he was made Count of Grand Riviere du Nord. After the kingdom was abolished, Riche aligned with the republic and president Boyer remaining commander of the north.

In March 1846, the rebel army proclaimed Riche president. Unlike his immediate predecessors he was an active president. He restored the Constitution of 1816 (with minor revisions) and transformed the Council of State into the Senate. The rule by decree of his immediate predecessors was reversed, and the government functioned in a constitutional framework. His administration was effective and ministers capable. During Riche's tenure, the Piquets rose again under their leader Aacau. They were subdued and order restored. In 1847, while visiting the northern province Riche unexpectedly died.[114]

In the years between 1844 after the fall of Boyer until 1847

---

113. Léger, Jacques Nicolas (1907). *Haiti: Her History and Her Detractors.* The Neale Publishing Company.

114. Trouillot, Henok. "La Republique d'Haiti Entre La Francophonie et l'americanisme (19è Siecle et Debut Du 20è)." Revista de Historia de América, no. 80 (1975): 87–145

the country had four presidents. Two died in office and two were overthrown. There was instability in the country as two groups vied for control. The Boyer faction ruled through the older veterans of the war of Independence (Guerrier and Riche). They were bitterly opposed by Rivière-Hérard and his supporters. This period was marked by instability and political violence toward the opposition. The Piquet uprisings were brutally suppressed. Under the Council of State, the opposition was treated with the heavy hand of repression. Gone were the days of Pétion and Boyer who tolerated their political opponents with a velvet touch.

18

CONTEXT

IT FELL UPON the Senate to elect the president to replace Riche. Outsiders who have written about Haiti's history tend to treat this period as one dominated by various dictators. But, the election of the president was conducted by the Senate in accord with the then constitution. Soulouque was chosen on the eighth ballot.[115] Until then, he had failed to receive more than one vote in a much-divided Senate. Several presidents chosen were seen as mere figureheads. The pattern was to select a popular general who had a role in both the war of independence and a politically prominent role after.

---

115. Dorsainvil, Dr. J. C. "Manuel Histoire D'Haiti" Editions Henri Deschamps; Portus Principis, 15 July 1934

Contrary to what some have written, Haiti was not governed by one long succession of dictators. There were powerful factions led by Senators who made and unmade presidents. Often, the real power was controlled and exercised by those in the Senate, and ministers appointed to run the government. The executive branch wielded much authority and sometimes operated outside constitutional boundaries. From 1844–46 there was no adherence to a constitution.

In 1846 Riche restored constitutional order and the Council of State was sworn in as the Senate. Haiti was thus restored to the status of a constitutional republic. The political elites that had governed since the time of independence vied for power. These factions did not coalesce as political parties. Many fell under the sway of charismatic, domineering, military figures.

Putting things in context, the political order of Europe favored the restoration of monarchy in France and absolutist rule throughout much of the rest of Europe. The English can be deemed the most democratic of governments at that time. When looking at the region, there was colonial rule in Caribbean and independent republics of Latin America. Some of these republics operated as did Haiti with a strong executive from a ruling elite. Some of these leaders were heavy handed and dictatorial. The transfer of power from one president to the next was often the result of a popular uprising leading to the assumption of power by a prominent general or politician through force or the threat of such.

In North America, Canada remained a colony of Great Britain. In the United States there was limited suffrage, peaceful transfer of power, established political parties, freedom of speech and assembly and a bill of rights that protected the freedom of a certain portion of the population. But the U.S. was no beacon of democracy at that time. The slavocracy in the Southern states was one of the most oppressive regimes of the modern era. Slavery, the dehumanization and exploitation of human populations on the basis of race, was still practiced in much of the world.

Haiti's politics of the period needs to be assessed in the context of the times. That we had a ruling elite that elected/selected the president of the republic after a long, drawn-out balloting process passes for as much democracy as was then known in the world. The president was chosen pursuant to a constitutional framework. The transfer of power was peaceful. The election/selection was not rigged; several candidates were considered. There was no slavery in Haiti. The people were free. Most of the population were peasants living in the rural countryside, many of whom owned and tilled their land. This was in stark contrast to the large latifundias of Latin America where the "peones" neither controlled their lives or destinies.

Most of Haiti's politics were practiced in Port-au-Prince and the large coastal cities. The daily life of the average Haitian was not directly impacted by whoever was president at the time. By and large left alone, the peasants often had a better deal than their counterparts in the region. For those of African descent living in the Western Hemisphere at that time, Haiti was as good as it got, far better than how those of African descent were treated in the United States and in Latin America.

Outsiders often suggest that Haiti was ruled by a succession of dictators from the time of our independence. That is a very superficial analysis, that perpetuates a falsehood. Indeed, it plays into a narrative promoted by those with an interest in projecting Haiti as a failure. The notion that formerly enslaved could rebel, revolt and secure their independence through a bloody war was anathema to slavocratic circles. Haiti was used to prove that those of African descent were not able to govern ourselves and had no real capacity to offer freedom or a better life to our citizens. We tell our story in a different and accurate way. During this time, the U.S. enslaved a significant part of its population, and was forcibly removing its first inhabitants from their ancestral lands.

19

SOULOUQUE

In March 1847, Faustin Soulouque was elected president of Haiti. Born enslaved in 1782 in Petit Goave, he was freed by the emancipation decree issued by Sonthonax in 1793. He joined the army of independence in 1803 and was a respected soldier rising to the rank of lieutenant by 1806. He was appointed to the Horse Guards under Pétion in 1810, and for the next four decades served as an officer in the Haitian army. He served in the Presidential guard under Boyer and rising to the rank of colonel during the presidency of Guerrier. He was viewed as loyal, dutiful, modest and, most important, apolitical. Under Riche, he was promoted to the highest rank in the Haitian military at that time, head of the Presidential guard.[116]

His perceived lack of interest in matters political was among the reasons that his name was considered by the Senate. The Boyerists who had made and unmade presidents thought they could control him. Soulouque was viewed as dull and ignorant, and thought to be easily malleable. He could barely read or write, and they felt he was ripe to play the role of puppet.[117] He had to be convinced to accept his election to the Presidency.

At first, he appeared to play the role of puppet. He kept the cabinet ministers in place and pursued the policies of the Riche government. Then Soulouque began to assert himself and exercise power.[118] He began by replacing certain ministers and by pressuring those suspected of conspiring against his regime. By April 1848 those who had brought Soulouque to power began to conspire against him. Some took up arms. His response was immediate and violent. He ordered the military to open fire on protesters. There was also a confrontation with Celigny Ardouin a powerful senator of the Boyer faction that had been responsible for electing Soulouque. Ardouin, accused of conspiring against Soulouque was arrested. Over

116. Baur, John E. "Faustin Soulouque, Emperor of Haiti His Character and His Reign." The Americas 6, no. 2 (1949): 131–66.

117. ibid

118. MacLeod, Murdo J. "The Soulouque Regime in Haiti, 1847–1859: A Reevaluation." *Caribbean Studies* 10, no. 3 (1970): 35–48.

the next few days there was open season on those who either were supporters of Ardouin or suspected of supporting him. It made no difference. They were indiscriminately massacred.[119]

The foreign consulates were filled with those escaping the terror. Until this point in time politics were not a blood sport. Though there were uprisings and armed suppression of the Piquets and Aacau, for the most part those in opposition were allowed to go into exile. The use of massacres and terror had only been practiced by Dessalines and Christophe. Haitian politics up until then were mostly bereft of terror and political repression. Soulouque brought things to a whole new level.

Soulouque introduced the "Zinglins" to Haiti. This group of Soulouque loyalists functioned as a private army and were used to carry out the most violent acts of repression against the political enemies of his regime.[120]

DOMINICAN CAMPAIGNS

After declaring its independence from Haiti in 1844, the Dominican Republic was not immediately recognized as an independent nation by the European powers. Some members

---

119. Baur, John E. (1949). "Faustin Soulouque, Emperor of Haiti His Character and His Reign": 143

120. Rogozinski, Jan (1999). *A Brief History of the Caribbean (Reviseded.)*. New York: Facts on File, Inc. pp. 220

of the governing class were not reconciled to the fact that the island was divided. There were constant troubles on the border with the Haitians maintaining troops that were harassed by the Dominicans.[121]

In 1848, the government of France recognized the independence of the Dominican Republic. Soulouque saw this as an infringement on the affairs of Haiti and took action. He led an invasion army in March 1849. The Haitian army had initial success against the Dominicans but were thwarted at the River Ocoa. There the Haitian army faced stiff resistance and Soulouque gave the order for a retreat that turned into a rout. The once vaunted army of Haiti was ultimately defeated. Upon his return to the capital, the defeated army and its president were hailed as heroes and feted by the populace.

On two subsequent occasions in 1850–51 Soulouque invaded the Dominican Republic. There was opposition from France, Great Britain and the United States so Soulouqe pulled back. In 1855 he threatened again with an army of 30,000 and was again defeated by the Dominican general Pedro Santana. The incursions into the Dominican Republic wreaked havoc on the nation's finances. For some the invasions were not popular, and the morale of the troops was low. After Soulouque no

121. Scheina, Robert L. (2003). *Latin America's Wars.* Potomac Books.

other Haitian president led an army of invasion to reclaim the eastern part of the island. The independence of the Dominican Republic was a reality that could not be overturned by the force of arms. Soulouque learned a bitter lesson.[122]

SECOND EMPIRE

In August 1849, shortly after the disastrous Dominican campaign, a petition began circulating in the lower Chamber to consolidate all public institutions in the hands of the executive and to have the president declared emperor. Matters moved quickly, and an imperial constitution was promulgated the following month. Haiti was declared an empire and Soulouque became Faustin I, the emperor of Haiti. A nobility was created with Soulouque's close collaborators granted noble titles. He was crowned emperor in April 1852 in a grand and costly ceremony inspired by the coronation of Napoleon I.[123]

An empire needed a nobility. Soulouque created a nobility that consisted of 4 princes, 59 dukes, 2 marquis, 99 counts, 215 barons and scores of other knights and lesser nobility. This was patterned after the First French Empire of Napoleon; it

---

122. Baur, John E. (1949). "Faustin Soulouque, Emperor of Haiti His Character and His Reign"

123. Davis, H. P. *Black Democrac –The Story of Haiti,* Read Books, 2008, p. 161

was also a way to reward those loyal to his regime. The new nobility also included the old nobility under Dessalines and Christophe, and the old titles were recognized.

END OF EMPIRE

In 1858, the Duc de Tabara, General Fabre Nicolas Geffrard led an insurrection against Soulouque. Even though he had been a loyal supporter of the Emperor, Geffrard who was popular in his own right lost favor and was under suspicion. Fearing the worst, Geffrard went to Gonaives and met with other opponents of the regime and began a revolution to replace Soulouque and restore the Republic. Geffrard led an army that defeated the emperor in battle. In January 1859, Geffrard entered Port-au-Prince in triumph and was proclaimed president of the republic.[124]

It should be noted that the second Haitian Empire was established in 1849, and three years later Louis-Napoleon the prince-president of France was proclaimed Napoleon III, emperor of the French. France had its second empire at the same time as Haiti. Press freedom under Napoleon III was restricted, and any criticism of the emperor was curtailed. The

---

124. Rogozinski, Jan (1999). *A Brief History of the Caribbean (Reviseded)*. New York: Facts on File, Inc. pp. 220

French opposition to Napoleon III used criticism of Faustin I as a clever way to attack Napoleon III. Faustin I was harshly ridiculed and portrayed as a buffoon. This derisive way of portraying our country humiliated Haitian sensibility. Many came to despise the emperor, empire and the regime in general.

LEGACY

Soulouque will go down as one of the most powerful rulers of Haiti. Ruling from 1847 to 1859 he was among one of the longest serving rulers. He ruled by violence and terror, forcibly eliminating his opponents via his private army the Zinglins. His three unsuccessful and costly invasions of the Dominican Republic wreaked havoc on the economy. The country could ill afford the expenses of his coronation.

Soulouque is remembered for the empire he proclaimed, and how he ruled. Unlike those who had ruled before him, power rested with him and was wielded without constraints.[125] The second empire contributed to the trajectory of Haiti's history. Within the first half-century of independence we had two emperors (Jacques I and Faustin I), one king (Henri 1ier), a president for life (Pétion) and a host of other presidents along

---

125. Dorsainvil, Dr. J. C. "Manuel Histoire D'Haiti" Editions Henri Deschamps; Portus Principis, 15 July 1934

with several constitutions. Leaving us a legacy that is unlike that of our neighbors.

From thereon, Haiti has been a constitutional republic led by a president. The executive branch has been the primary source of power. The other branches-the legislature and judiciary-have exercised power and authority as a complement to the executive rather than as a balancer or mitigant to the executive.

Haiti's detractors have asserted that we have been ruled by a succession of dictators.

That misrepresents Haiti's historical reality and comes from several camps. Contemporary observers with an interest in maintaining the slave system continually portrayed us in the most negative light. They could be counted upon to describe Haiti as always having been governed by dictators. Unlike our neighbors, we had to constantly face the negative press that came from a source with a vested interest in seeing our experiment in self-rule falter.

More modern observers of Haiti's long history have not been all that interested in the period between our glorious independence and the onerous U.S. occupation that befell our country in the early 20th century. The years in between are described in a most cursory way, and one gets the impression that to these observers that period of time is but a blur. Most if not all of these observers fail to analyze Haiti at that time and place its history in context. When compared to the other Latin American republics, Haiti's experience is similar.

After Bolivar, the vast majority of the newly minted Latin American Republics were ruled by various presidents in an unfettered manner.[126] Executive authority went unchallenged by the other branches of government. Some of the presidents ruled by violence and terror. Others were more benign. Just like in Haiti, the political elite took an active role in politics, and rulers were drawn from that class. Most of the population was left out of the political system. These elites coalesced around personalities. Political parties evolved around a powerful set of actors. Power rested with the president and those who supported him. That was the nature of politics in the region. Historians of these other nations have not generalized away a period by referring to a long list of dictators who ruled.

After Soulouque, some issues were resolved. For one, Haiti would never have a king or emperor at its head. The political actors accepted that the Haitian state would function as a republic.[127] Second, there would be no further attempt to invade our neighbor to the east. The desire to govern the whole island

---

126. ibid

as one nation and country ran its course. Henceforth, Haitian presidents and the political elites came to move past the dream of a one-island nation united and indivisible. Indeed, it became an existential tenet of Haitian policy to maintain the independence of the Dominican Republic.

127. Davis, H. P. *Black Democracy – The Story of Haiti,* Read Books, 2008, p. 161

20

FIRST HALF-CENTURY

THE FALL OF THE SECOND EMPIRE ended that period where the heroes of independence dominated our politics. The first decade of our independence was a bloody affair with Dessalines instituting violence and revenge toward the French who remained in the newly independent Black nation. After Dessalines, the country was divided into a kingdom in the north and a republic in the west and south.[128] For most of the decade the battle for control was waged. Ultimately the republican ideal prevailed

---

128. Dorsainvil, Dr. J. C. "Manuel Histoire D'Haiti" Editions Henri Deschamps; Portus Principis, 15 July 1934

Christophe, endowed with talent, charisma and vision, was unable to work alongside the other powerful generals who had just rid themselves of one tyrant and were not going to fall under the thumb of another. The schism was partly based on personalities. But there also were competing visions of how to secure the independence and viability of the new nation. Pétion proved to be a more astute political operator and in the end, won out. The Haitian republic served as a sort of midwife to the independence movements of Latin America.[129] That is a significant achievement that has been too little noticed. Haiti as a haven for all enslaved was a vision that was articulated and put into practice.

Our independence was both a thorn in the side of the enslavers, and rebuke to those who denigrated those of African descent. Independence gained on the battlefield had to be defended in the diplomatic salon. A controversial treaty along with an onerous indemnity was signed with France to assure that France would not seek to reconquer its former colony.

Each such assertion of independence came a price that no other nation in the Western Hemisphere had to pay. We paid in blood and then treasure to secure our independence. The signal achievement of the first 50 years was to secure the

---

129. ibid

independence of the young nation. We ended that period by being the only independent nation in the Caribbean but not the only one in Latin America. There were other young nations like ours. The independence wave had taken hold and neither Spain nor France could reconquer former colonies. We were not alone, but we were the first.

The first half-century of our independence was both tumultuous and consequential. One can debate the extent to which Haiti contributed to the cause of Latin American independence, but what cannot be debated was that El Libertador was given shelter, arms, munitions and men to continue the struggle. Only one condition was imposed: that the enslaved must be freed.[130]

The fractious internal struggles of our first two decades created an inward focus. When stability was restored, the Boyer government ruled over the entire island and projected Haitian influence beyond our borders. Haiti stood as a beacon to others of African descent in the Western Hemisphere. The support for Greek independence, albeit quite modest, again represented a role on the world stage for this small emerging nation. We held the moral high ground. For a time, we stood

---

130. Dorsainvil, Dr. J. C. "Manuel Histoire D'Haiti" Editions Henri Deschamps; Portus Principis, 15 July 1934

alone with no allies and many enemies. Maintaining our independence for the first half-century was no small achievement.

21

NOIRS V. MULÂTRES

APART FROM the one continuous dictatorship canard that has been used to describe Haiti's history the other has been the noir v. mulâtres dichotomy. This racialized prism through which our history is viewed reeks of intellectual laziness and inaccuracy. Prior to our independence there was indeed a clear distinction between noirs and mulâtres as established by the enslavers. The bloody civil war led by Andre Rigaud has been described as a war between the mulâtres of the south and Toussaint and the army of the noirs.[131] The army of independence defies that dichotomy. Our national motto "L'Union Fait La Force" underscores that there was no

---

131. Rogozinski, Jan (1999). *A Brief History of the Caribbean* (revised.). New York: Facts on File, Inc.

distinction among groups heretofore treated as separate. The Haitian flag was established when Dessalines tore out the white from the tri-color flag of France and united the Noirs (blue) and mulâtres (red) under the banner of Haiti.

There is a saying among Haitians that a mulâtre without money is considered a noir, and a noir with money is considered a mulâtre. There exists a fluidity to the physical appearance of individuals that belies any clear lines of distinction. Moreover, within every camp there were Noirs and mulâtres on each side. Each of the supposed Mulâtre presidents were supported by prominent Noirs, and vice versa. It is more accurate to reflect Haiti's history as being marked by a class system where the elites are comprised of both categories of Haitians. It is also true that many more Mulâtres are represented in the ruling elite than in the general population.

What is often ignored in the presentation of these divisions is that in a rather small country such as Haiti the governing class or elites have intermingled in a way as to blur the lines that are presented. For example, the descendants of Toussaint and Dessalines to name but a few became leading members of "bourgeois mulâtre society"[132] Moreover, within certain

---

132. Dorsainvil, Dr. J. C. "Manuel Histoire D'Haiti" Editions Henri Deschamps; Portus Principis, 15 July 1934

families there are branches that are considered Noirs whereas other are seen as mulâtres. This fluidity and intermingling points to the ideological prejudices of certain authors or the moment in history in which a particular author has lived. For example, those authors who view history through the prism of socialism or Marxism have tended to focus on the class struggle. Yet Haiti had never had a proletariat. So, the Haitian peasant has been seen as a proxy for the proletariat.

Other authors view Haiti's history through the prism of race and thus seek to categorize in a most imperfect way. There are a number of Haitian leaders, presidents and prominent figures whose physical appearance defies the noir/mulâtre dichotomy presented by authors operating under a racialized prism.

In our history and the telling of it, the differences have been less about race than about the personalities. The richness of our history has come from the characters that have appeared on the scene: brilliant, mediocre to, plain incompetent. As in other countries they have competed for political power and control. In the case of Haiti, the rise of an individual to power has been supported by a group of acolytes who supported the individual. Those acolytes typically had family and regional ties to the person or group in power. To assert that the main division was based on race fails since the governing elite came from the same class, regardless of skin tone or personal appearance.

The majority of our leading citizens have been drawn from the same class of individuals since the days of independence.[133] Ties of family and region have been more important than those of skin tone or appearance. Thus, when we recount our story, the narrative is about the acts of the leading protagonists, with a focus on the people and their actions.

---

133. Dorsainvil, Dr. J. C. "Manuel Histoire D'Haiti" Editions Henri Deschamps; Portus Principis, 15 July 1934

22

RESTORATION of THE REPUBLIC

A
FTER THE END of the Second Haitian Empire, Fabre Nicolas Geffrard was elected president of the Republic of Haiti. Born in 1806, he represented a new generation of Haitian leaders never to have known anything other than an independent country. His father was a general in the army of independence and a signatory to the Act of Independence. Geffrard, a supporter of Riviere-Herard, fought in the ranks of the troops that deposed Boyer. Promoted to the rank of general, he was popular, cutting a handsome figure on horseback and known for his equestrian ability. Stories have been told of Geffrard rescuing a child while in full gallop.

His popularity and political affiliation with Riviere-Herard brought him under suspicion by President Riche who had him court-martialed for misconduct. He was acquitted by a council of war presided over by Soulouque and became a close collaborator of Soulouque's. Rising to the highest ranks of the military and court under the Second Empire. Geffrard was at once the Duke of Tabara (he had won a military victory at La Tabarra) and the chief of staff of the military. As a military man, he acquitted himself admirably in the failed invasions of the Dominican Republic and was even wounded in battle. A favorite of Soulouque, some have suggested that he manipulated the emperor to his benefit. As with others in the close company of the paranoid Soulouque he ultimately fell under suspicion. Fearing for his well-being, he led the insurrection that removed Soulouque.[134]

Unlike his predecessor, Géffrard exuded a calm demeanor and did not employ terror as a tool to maintain and exercise power. He kept many prominent figures of the Soulouque regime in their positions and even kept all of the chamber of deputies. This was an astute way to consolidate power. Slowly but surely, Géffrard began to remove these individuals, replacing them with men loyal to him.

---

134. Alaux, Gustave d'. "La Révolution Haïtienne de 1859: Chute De L'empereur Soulouque. Le Président Geffrard." *Revue Des Deux Mondes (1829–1971)* 23, no. 2 (1859): 341–92.

He reduced the size of the army from 30,000 to 15,000. He formed his own presidential guard and trained them himself. Thus, he assured himself of having control over the armed forces and, most importantly, the presidential guard. The latter served as a springboard for Soulouque to rise to power. Géffrard brought into his government newer better educated and more competent breed. The Elie-Dubois brothers represent an example of the ministers that were involved in Géffrad's government.

Education was one area where Géffrard made his mark.[135] A law school was founded in 1859, and the medical school that was begun by Boyer was reinstituted. Schools of music and art were established during his tenure. Schools in such cities as Jacmel, Jérémie, St. Marc and Gonaives were both established and modernized. Young promising Haitians were sent to Europe on government scholarships to conclude their studies. From that time on Haitian governments have sponsored generations of young Haitians in their studies abroad. As a result, Haiti's intellectual elite has left quite a mark.[136]

---

135. Logan, Rayford W. "Education in Haiti." *The Journal of Negro History* 15, no. 4 (1930): 401–60.

136. Dorsainvil, Dr. J. C. " Manuel Histoire D'Haiti" Editions Henri Deschamps; Portus Principis, 15 July 1934

CONCORDAT

One of the most lasting achievements of the Géffrard administration was the 1860 signing of the Concordat with the Vatican, an important step concluding a process begun by the Boyer administration. Thus, was assured the formal recognition of Haiti by the Vatican and for the organization of the Catholic Church in Haiti.[137] Though voodoo was and remains the religion practiced by the majority of the Haitian population, Catholicism planted deep roots in Haiti and became the official religion. The Haitian government received and obtained a diocese, a resident bishop and parishes. Haiti was treated on par with the other Catholic nations.

DOMINICAN REPUBLIC

The Dominican Republic was established in 1844 after obtaining its independence from Haiti. Several parties vied for power and the country remained fractured. The main fault line lay with a group that sought the protection of a European power (France or England) or even the United States as a means of countering the threat of a Haitian invasion. Under Soulouque, Haiti did indeed invade the Dominican Republic to unify the

---

137. Clorméus, Lewis Ampidu. "Les Stratégies de Lutte Contre La «superstition» En Haïti Au XIXe Siècle." *Journal of Haitian Studies* 20, no. 2 (2014): 104–25.

island under Haitian control. The other main faction wanted to remain free of foreign intervention.

In 1861, Pedro Santana, then president of the Republic did something that few leaders would have done, he invited Spain to return and take control of its former colony. This act both changed the nature of the Dominican state from an independent nation to a colony of Spain, and the balance of power on the island. The Haitian government under Geffrard had signed a five-year truce with the Dominican Republic. The return of Spain represented a threat to the independence of Haiti.

Géffrard's government responded by providing support to the Dominican faction that favored independence. The Dominican patriots were given shelter and support by Haiti. From our territory in 1863, they launched what became their second war of independence. Yet again, Haiti had come to the aid of a neighbor seeking to regain its independence from Spain. By 1865 the Spanish left the island for good.

USA

Haitians supported the abolitionist movement in the United States. As was the case during the Boyer administration, Geffrard's government encouraged immigration of

African Americans to Haiti. A small group of immigrants led by the Reverand James Theodore Holly moved to and remained in Haiti. We saw ourselves as defending those of African descent in the New World. The harsh conditions of slavery and discrimination that prevailed in North America were denounced. When the famous abolitionist John Brown was executed, a state funeral with full honors was held on his behalf.

During the U.S. Civil War, Haiti was among the few nations in the Caribbean fully in support of the Union cause. The Spanish and British colonies of Cuba and the Bahamas openly supported the Confederates and harbored blockade runners and contrabanders. In contrast, the U.S. Navy was welcome in Haitian waters and used Cap-Haitien as the headquarters of its West Indian Squadron. That was critical in maintaining the Union blockade of the Florida Straits.[138] Haiti exported cotton to the Union states and increased its commercial ties to the United States.

In recognition of Haiti's support for the Union, diplomatic relations were formally established in 1862. In addition to the changing relations with the Dominican Republic, the formal

138. Seraille, William. "Afro-American Emigration to Haiti during the American Civil War." *The Americas* 35, no. 2 (1978): 185–200.

recognition of Haiti by the United States was an achievement by the Géffrard government. This meant the end of the diplomatic isolation. The ports of Haiti became open to foreign commerce. Trade with the United States, France and Great Britain increased dramatically. Haiti engaged more fully with the outside world.[139]

In foreign affairs, Géffrard signed a Concordat with the Vatican, opened diplomatic relations with the United States and provided assistance to Dominican patriots. Here were three concrete results that came from the change in world view and policies pursued by Géffrard. That the Dominican Republic would remain an independent neighboring country was a major about face from the bellicose position taken by his predecessor. The conclusion of the Concordat with the Vatican was the culmination of a long process, initiated decades prior. Relations with the United States was a major step to break the grip of isolation that plagued our first-half century.

DOMESTIC POLITICS

The legislative elections of 1862 and 1863 ushered in the 10th and 11th legislatures in our history. These were not the

---

139. Baur, John E. "The Presidency of Nicolas Geffrard of Haiti." *The Americas* 10, no. 4 (1954): 425–61.

rubber-stamp legislatures of past regimes and certainly not the 9th legislature under Soulouque. The elections of 1863 brought to office many deputies who were members of the opposition. Heretofore there had been few instances of any organized opposition, let alone deputies elected to the legislature with opposing points of view. The elections of 1863 were the freest in the annals of the young nation. One of the notable achievements of the 11th legislature was to restore a five-year term of office for the president.

OPPOSITION

As with all governments, there were opponents to Géffrard and his administration. Indeed, there were conspiracies and attempts to overthrow the government. These opponents were well known public officials and generals. The reaction of the government was often swift and immediate. Géffrard dealt with these opponents by capturing and executing them. There were too few instances of clemency to be seen as anything other than the exception. The resort to execution was lamentable and served to harden the opposition.

There were legislators whose opinions differed from the government and expressed these differences within the confines of the legislative branch and process. In contrast to the previous government (and this was no small step) there was active debate in the parliament. Those who opposed the government were not repressed. For example, the legislative session of 1862 saw open criticism of the Concordat, and in the session of 1863 the legislature stopped an attempt to allow foreigners to own property in Haiti. There are numerous examples of robust debate and opposition because of policies. Géffrard, was once accused of aspiring to become a dictator,[140] replied in an address to the legislature defending his government and record. There was space for debate and give and take with the legislative branch. Opposition expressed within the bounds of the institutional framework was indeed tolerated. Attempts at overthrowing the government were dealt with harshly.

Among the most menacing opponents of Géffrard was Sylvain Salnave, a popular politician from the north with a great following among the population. In 1865, Salnave headed an attempt to overthrow the government and succeeded in taking control of Cap-Haitien. Géffrard responded by personally directing a siege and blockade of Cap-Haitien. The British navy assisted in the siege. In the end, Salnave escaped to the Dominican Republic, and order was restored.

---

140. Dorsainvil, Dr. J. C. "Manuel Histoire D'Haiti" Editions Henri Deschamps; Portus Principis, 15 July 1934

It took six months to recapture Cap-Haitien and restore order. The expenses of maintain a standing army represented a drain on the nation's resources. There was a great deal of resentment, and in some sectors of the population the government lost favor. This was a turning point. Salnave had weakened and even mortally wounded Géffard's government. Regional rivalries that had laid dormant for decades reemerged. This was the beginning of the end.

In January of 1867, another attempt to overthrow the government was hatched. This time it came from within the ranks of the Tiralleurs (the vaunted Presidential Guard). The attempt was put down with fatalities. That dissent leading to revolt came from the ranks of his own Presidential Guard shook Géffrard. He tried a soft hand and declared a general amnesty, and even made concessions to the legislature. It was too little too late. Months later the last and successful revolt was begun. Geffrard saw the writing on the wall, resigned, and went into exile in Jamaica.[141]

LEGACY

Géffard is one of Haiti's greatest presidents. There were tangible achievements, and a sea change in how he governed.

___

141. Baur, John E. "The Presidency of Nicolas Geffrard of Haiti." *The Americas* 10, no. 4 (1954): 425–61.

The use of terror and political assassination (via the use of the Zinglins) came to an abrupt halt. The emphasis on education and the creation of the law school, re-instituting the medical school was much needed in the country. In addition, new schools were founded throughout the country. The Géffrard administration also sent abroad young Haitians to complete their studies.

In the realm of foreign policy, the country's isolation was addressed with the signing of Concordat with the Vatican bringing Haiti into the fold of other Catholic nations. Diplomatic relations were established with the United States in recognition of Haitian support for the Union cause. The relationship with the Dominican Republic was set on a new course. Under Géffrard, Haiti's isolation ended and relations with our immediate neighbors[142] were redefined and established with the United States.

The change in policy with the Dominican Republic was irreversible and came to be accepted that Dominican independence was in Haiti's best interest. In fact, Haitians recognized that the loss of independence by the Dominican Republic would threaten Haiti's own independence. The relationship with the United States removed one of the principal actors

---

142. Dorsainvil, Dr. J. C. "Manuel Histoire D'Haiti" Editions Henri Deschamps; Portus Principis, 15 July 1934

in the diplomatic isolation of Haiti. Haiti provided material support both to the Union during the U.S. Civil War and to the Dominican patriots who fought to restore Dominican independence.

The economy prospered for a time as exports of our agricultural products increased significantly. Our ports, closed to foreign trade, were opened. Haitians benefited from the trade that ensued. Haiti made progress, in many areas as a consequence of Géffrard's policies.

23

INSURRECTIONS AND DEBT

BY THE END of Géffrard's administration the nation's finance were a mess.[143] In part this was caused by the massive unforeseen expenditures relating to the siege of Cap-Haitien. An army was kept in the field for a period of six months with costs not part of any budget that had been approved. Other priorities were shortchanged in order to put down the rebellion.

Throughout our history the changeover in governments has not proceeded along the established constitutional norms. In fact, insurrection has been the preferred route. Each such insurrection had to be financed with loans taken out by the

---

143. Dorsainvil, Dr. J. C. "Manuel Histoire D'Haiti" Editions Henri Deschamps; Portus Principis, 15 July 1934

insurgents. Once the insurgents had taken over the government, those obligations became obligations of the new government. The creditors for these loans were foreign merchants who in turn required favorable treatment on the part of the new government. So, trade concessions were made available to those merchants. In addition, the debt incurred by the insurgents had to be refinanced by the new government in foreign capital markets. Terms were less than favorable to Haiti. Moreover, existing loans were already a burden to the Haitian economy. When one considers that Haiti was required by treaty to pay an indemnity to France for recognition of our independence, the new loans were a crippling burden.

Funds that could otherwise be available for developing roads, building schools or other initiatives were deployed instead toward debt service and repayment. Thus, was created a structural handicap toward development.[144] The country's resources went to finance one insurrection after another. When graft and corruption are added to the mix, we can see that far fewer resources were spent on developing the country. Well intended governments and senior public officials were faced

---

144. Apuzzo, Matt; Méheut, Constant; Gebrekidan, Selam; Porter, Catherine (2022-05-20). "How a French Bank Captured Haiti". *The New York Times.*

with a handicap, Haiti's budget was already spoken for. In ensuing decades this pattern would repeat.

Haiti was by no means alone in this insurrection and debt dynamic. Most of the fledgling republics of Latin America faced the same conundrum and for similar reasons. What if all those funds had been diverted away from debt repayment and gone toward building infrastructure such as roads, and schools?

24

SALNAVE

SYLVAIN SALNAVE, born in Cap Haitien in 1827, enlisted in the army in 1850 as part of the cavalry. He supported Géffrard in the removal of Soulouqe and was promoted to major. Like the previous presidents or heads of state, he came from the ranks of the military. Like the others he served the head of state that he later deposed. This was the pattern for this period of our history where the military leader rose to political authority. Unlike many predecessors, Salnave became the darling of the masses. Wildly popular among the populace, he assiduously courted their support. This was outside the norm of Haitian politics at the time. Popular support was not a prerequisite to political advancement.[145]

---

145. Dorsainvil, Dr. J. C. "Manuel Histoire D'Haiti" Editions Henri Deschamps; Portus Principis, 15 July 1934

Salnave bitterly opposed Géffrard because he believed that the government did not do nearly enough to oppose the occupation of the Dominican Republic by Spain.[146] Salnave initiated several attempts to overthrow the government of Géffrard. In 1864 he led an uprising in the north that was put down. In 1866 he led another revolt and was again defeated. A year later Géffrard was deposed.

Even though Géffrard was overthrown, he still had allies in important positions. They were leery of Salnave and his popularity with the masses. A provisional government was convened with the Salnave among its leaders along with Nissage Saget and Victorin Chevalier. A constituent assembly was also put into place.

Salnave's entry into Port-au-Prince was met by an enthusiastic crowd of supporters. The capital had rarely seen this type of exuberant reception. This demonstration of support emboldened Salnave and his supporters. He withdrew from the provisional government and was acclaimed "Protector of the Republic." The constituent assembly, bowing to popular pressure declared Salnave, president of the republic. Salnave enjoyed being a soldier and head of the military more than being the head of a government or head of state.

---

146. Wilson, James Grant; Fiske, John (1898). Appletons' Cyclopaedia of American Biography: Pickering-Sumter. D. Appleton. p.378

The constituent assembly was dissolved, new elections held, and a new legislature was convened. Many of the elected representatives had been part of Géffrard's government. One of the unfortunate events that occurred upon Salnave's ascension to the presidency was the arrest without warrant of a Géffrard loyalist named Leon Montas. Highly regarded for his probity and ability, this general oversaw the north under Géffrard and was the one responsible for defeating Salnave in his failed insurrections. General Montas was imprisoned and ultimately died there.

The legislature put pressure on the government regarding the fate of General Montas. Salnave's supporters broke into the chamber and ransacked the parliament, suppressing its work. The legislative session lasted but eleven days. The shock and outrage at this breach of decorum and attempt to intimidate the legislature led to fervent opposition to Salnave.

CACOS

The Cacos[147] were a group of peasants from the north organized by their local chieftains. They operated with powerful politicians of the region to take control of events and overthrow the government. The first rising of the Cacos occurred

---

147. Léger, Jacques Nicolas (1907). *Haiti, Her History and Her Detractors.* Neale Publishing Company. pp. 211–216.

under Salnave's government. His opponents paid and armed the local chieftains to raise an armed group. Salnave led his army against the Cacos and was defeated.

PIQUETS

The southern equivalent of the Cacos were armed irregulars drawn from the disaffected southern peasants. Salnave was besieged from the north and south. He fought doggedly and relied upon his popular support in Port-au-Prince. In the end he was outnumbered. The prominent generals who had supported him such as Victorin Chevalier joined the rebels, depriving Salnave of his best general. In addition, leading figures such as Nissage Saget, Boisron Canal and Nord Alexis (each became president) coalesced to drive Salnave from power. He fled to the Dominican Republic to regroup with supporters.

The Dominican government, under pressure from the Haitian government, detained Salnave and handed him over to the Haitian authorities. He was sent back to Port-au-Prince as a prisoner.[148] This was unprecedented since most previously deposed presidents moved on in exile and were hardly heard from again. But Salnave was conspiring to regain the presidency. His opponents resolved to neutralize him as a

---

148. ibid

political force. Tried by a revolutionary tribunal, he was found guilty of murder, arson and violating the Constitution. He was sentenced to death and faced a firing squad.

Salnave was the first president of Haiti to have faced execution.[149] Unlike Dessalines who was assassinated by ambush, and Christophe who took his own life before the mob could do its worst, Salnave was tried and executed. Despite his popularity, he managed to antagonize and unite the political elite against him. Even the Catholic Church openly opposed his government. With enemies aplenty, he met a fate unique in our history.

---

149. Dorsainvil, Dr. J. C. "Manuel Histoire D'Haiti" Editions Henri Deschamps; Portus Principis, 15 July 1934

Toussaint L'Ouverture (1743-1803)

Jean Jacques Dessalines (1758-1806)

HENRI CHRISTOPHE (1767-1820)

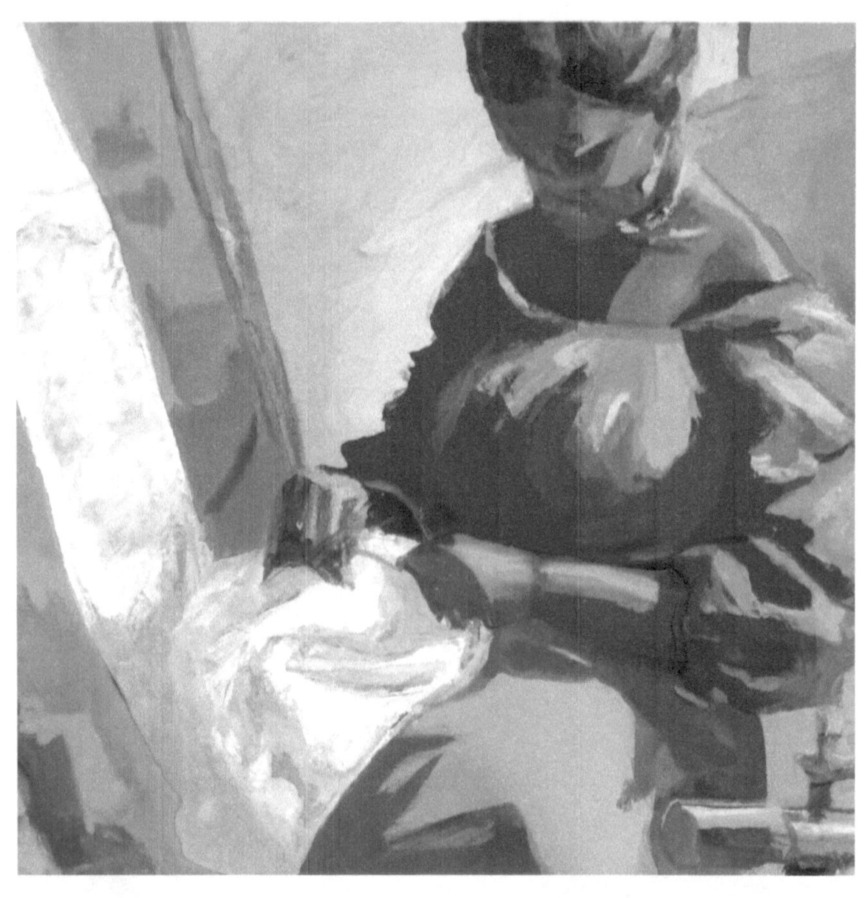

CATHERINE FLON (1772-1831)

MARIE LOUISE COIDAVID (1778-1851)

ALEXANDRE PÉTION (1770-1818)

JEAN-PIERRE BOYER (1776-1850)

MARIE-MADELEINE LACHENAIS (1778-1843)

FAUSTIN SOULOUQUE (1782-1867)

ÉLISABETH ADÉLINA DÉRIVAL LÉVÊQUE OR
ADÉLINA SOULOUQUE (1820-1878)

FABRE NICOLAS GEFFRARD (1806-1878)

Jean-Nicolas Nissage Saget (1810-1880)

PIERRE THÉOMA BOISROND-CANAL (1832-1905)

LYSIUS SALOMON (1815-1888)

FLORVIL HYPPOLITE (1828-1896)

FRANÇOIS C. ANTOINE SIMON (1843-1923)

Pierre Nord Alexis (1820-1910)

ANTÉNOR FIRMIN (1850-1911)

HAMMERTON KILLICK (1856-1902)

25

DEMOCRATIC INTERLUDE

A FTER SALNAVE, a provisional government was installed with General Nissage Saget at its head along with Michel Domingue and Nord Alexis as other prominent members of what became known as the Council of State.[150] One of the first acts of the provisional government was to recognize the constitution 1867 and organize elections for the legislature. The new parliament was elected and met in March of 1870. Nissage Saget was elected president for a four-year term in accord with the constitution.

The period during which Saget ruled was unique for our country. In fact, this period can be seen as a democratic

---

150. Du Bois, W.E.B., and Robert Gregg. *The Negro*. University of Pennsylvania Press, 2001. http://www.jstor.org/stable/j.ctt1287p46.

interlude. Saget was known for his restraint in his use of power and observed the rule of law. Unlike many of his predecessors his term was marked by adherence to the constitution. Saget, imprisoned for a long period under Soulouque did not treat his opponents in the same fashion. There were attempts to overthrow the government especially in Cap-Haitien that had been a hotbed of support for Salnave.

After one revolt was put down, Saget went to Cap-Haitien to remind the citizens that when Pétion was president he had also faced insurrection. In his magnanimity, Pétion burned all records and documents implicating those who had conspired against his government. Saget said that he too was in possession of letters implicating those who had conspired against his government. Unlike Pétion, he declared, he would not destroy those records. The Capois got the message. In the end, Saget didn't pursue his opponents, and no actions were taken against those suspected of conspiring against the government.[151]

Saget as president showed restraint unlike some predecessors. He worked with and respected the role of the legislature. The best example was the monetary reform of 1870. Both the executive and legislative branches agreed that the paper money

---

151. Dorsainvil, Dr. J. C. "Manuel Histoire D'Haiti" Editions Henri Deschamps; Portus Principis, 15 July 1934

introduced by the Salnave government had created problems for the economy because of its uncertain value.

Though there was consensus as to what needed to be done the pace of the reform needed was debated. The executive branch opted to introduce the new currency gradually with re-valuation whereas the legislature led by the Liberal Party stalwarts Boyer-Bazelais and Edmond Paul argued for a more drastic approach. This was a policy difference on a matter of substance., not opposition for opposition's sake as had been the case in our recent political history. Unlike past governments, the legislature had the authority to compel government ministers to appear and present their position.

As is the case in any democracy or functioning constitutional system, debates over substantive policies can be messy and protracted. Here it took two years and several ministers of finance for the executive branch to agree with the legislature. Paper money was replaced with copper coins whose value was more certain. Major legislation was passed, for monetary reform, within the bounds of the constitution and with support of both the executive and legislative branches. This was unchartered ground, and a considerable achievement.[152]

---

152. Léger, Jacques Nicolas (1907). *Haiti, Her History and Her Detractors*. Neale Publishing Company.

In foreign affairs the main issue that confronted Nissage Saget's administration was the attempt by the United States to annex the Dominican Republic.[153] In 1870 the U.S. government under Ulysses Grant entered into a treaty with the Dominican Republic to annex the latter into the U.S. By a narrow margin, the treaty failed to be ratified by the U.S. Senate. The opposition to the annexation was led by Senator Charles Sumner. Senator Sumner was feted in Haiti and awarded a gold medal for his efforts.

A Dominican faction led by Generals Luperon and Cabral strongly opposed this loss of independence. Consistent with the prior Haitian governments, this faction found support within Haiti.

This was the era of gunboat diplomacy. During the Franco-Prussian War of 1870, Haiti manifested its support for France. Germany emerged victorious. In 1872 two German gunboats appeared in the waters off Port-au-Prince demanding reparations for damages suffered by German merchants operating in Haiti. This was the first and not last incident of gunboat aggression on the part of the European powers toward Haiti and the neighboring republics of Latin America. Ultimately,

---

153. Dorsainvil, Dr. J. C. "Manuel Histoire D'Haiti" Editions Henri Deschamps; Portus Principis, 15 July 1934

the Saget government paid the reparations and suffered a humiliating setback. Haiti was powerless in the face of Germany's aggression.[154]

LEGISLATIVE POWER

In the Saget administration the first political party in the history of the nation was founded. The Liberal Party founded in 1870 by Jean-Pierre Boyer-Bazelais and Edmond Paul[155], had as its motto "le pouvoir au plus capable," loosely translated as those who are capable should rule. The idea was to have in positions of power those who were competent to do the job. Politics up to that time rewarded those who were loyal to the President regardless of ability. The party also emphasized the common African ancestry of all Haitians, thus resisting the tendency to divide the country. The rise of the Liberal Party led to the formation of the National Party which had as its motto "le pouvoir au plus grand nombre," with its loose translation that power should go to the greatest number.

Competing parties were represented in the parliament. This exercise of power was new to the country. Boyer-Bazelais and

---

154. Léger, Jacques Nicolas (1907). *Haiti, Her History and Her Detractors.* Neale Publishing Company.

155. Dorsainvil, Dr. J. C. "Manuel Histoire D'Haiti" Editions Henri Deschamps; Portus Principis, 15 July 1934

Septimus Rameau were towering figures in governing the country. Politicians who were not president wielded power. They raised the art of debate to levels not heretofore seen in our republic. This was a period of contested elections where the outcome was not preordained.

For the first time in our history, the executive branch had to share power with the legislature. The executive branch was held accountable, and ministers were required to obtain approval for the budget. There was oversight of the executive branch, and the constitution was observed.

This all too brief period in our history highlights a president who did not stifle, intimidate, or repress the political opposition. In contrast to most of his predecessors, Nissage Saget observed the constitution. His administration provided the citizens of Haiti with more political freedom then they had ever experienced. The ascendance of not one but two political parties with competing visions for the country was a novelty in our politics.

As his term ended in May of 1874, Nissage Saget got on his donkey and left Port-au-Prince and politics for good. He retired to St. Marc, living in tranquility until he passed away in 1880. Nissage Saget was the nation's first president to serve his term and retiring thereafter. Unlike his predecessors, he did not try to stay beyond the constitutionally mandated four-year term. Moreover, he arranged for a peaceful transition to the next president with a provisional government chaired by the head of the Haitian army Michel Domingue.[156]

In contrast to the verdicts that have been rendered about the nature of politics in our country, we can point to this period in our history to affirm that democracy was indeed practiced in Haiti in the 19th century. The Constitution was upheld, and the legislature played the role accorded to it by the constitution. There were two competing political parties offering different views of the way forward for the country. The elections were contested. Substantive policy differences that were debated.

The parliament held the executive branch accountable for the first time in our history. Politics were about more than just aligning with the most powerful individual. The oratory of the day was compelling and elevated. There was political freedom. Citizens enjoyed free speech and freedom of assembly. This all too brief period has not been appreciated enough; alas it did not last. The roots of democracy, not deeply planted were easily uprooted.

------

156. Léger, Jacques Nicolas (1907). *Haiti, Her History and Her Detractors*. Neale Publishing Company.

All of this happened under Saget. He deserves the credit for his moderation, and his respect for the constitution. For the first time in our history an opposition was allowed to function. The existence of influential and popular politicians who were not the president did not trouble Saget. The attempts to overthrow the government were put down and not followed by waves of terror or repression. The president opted for the velvet touch rather than the iron fist of his predecessors.

In our story Nissage Saget must be elevated to the first rank of our presidents. He showed us and our posterity that we can govern ourselves democratically. His ruled ended not in exile but to his home in peaceful retirement. He had played his role and had served his country. He stepped away for good.

26

OLD POLITICS

Saget's departure brought an end to the democratic interlude. It was politics as usual. But in this case Michel Domingue[157] was a figurehead president. The true ruler of Haiti was Septimus Rameau the vice president and nephew of the president. This wasn't a case of running things behind the scenes. To the contrary, Septimus Rameau was recognized as the power in Haiti. Domingue was an old soldier with neither the appetite nor aptitude for ruling a nation.

Septimus Rameau, a learned and prominent politician in his own right, was among the leading figures in the parliament during the administration of Nissage Saget. Rameau was vain

---

157. ibid

and intolerant of opposition. He kept his own counsel and had few political allies.

The most noteworthy achievement of the Domingue administration was the signing of a peace treaty with the Dominican Republic.[158] Independence for the Dominican Republic was now seen as to be a vital interest for Haiti. The meddling of foreign powers such as Spain and the United States represented a threat to our own hard-won independence. Rather than seeking to reclaim control of the eastern part of the island, public opinion had shifted. Haitians were sympathetic to the plight of the Dominicans who had seen their independence compromised and threatened.

The second event of note during the brief rule of Michel Domingue was the negotiation of a loan with France. The loan was concluded on terms unfavorable to the government. Allegations of fraud and corruption damaged the reputation of the government. Rameau's response was to silence his most vociferous critics. The opposition to the loans was led by Generals Pierre Momplaisir-Pierre, Broussais Brice and Boisrond-Canal.[159] The first two were accosted by the soldiers

---

158. Dorsainvil, Dr. J. C. "Manuel Histoire D'Haiti" Editions Henri Deschamps; Portus Principis, 15 July 1934

159. ibid

of the government. General Momplaisir-Pierre was at home and fought off the soldiers until he was killed. General Brice was shot at and wounded. He was able to secure political asylum at the Spanish consulate where he died of his wounds. Boisrond-Canal, the most fortunate, gained access to the U.S. consulate.

Other prominent opponents were targeted by the government and fled the country. The revulsion generated by this wanton political violence led to a general uprising against the government. The country as a whole revolted against the government. In the ensuing anarchy and violence, Rameau was killed and Domingue was able to escape as many had before him to Jamaica.[160]

In contrast to Nissage Saget who got on his donkey and went out of public life at the end of his presidential term, Domingue was only able to serve two years in office. The lamentable turn of events introduced a degree of violence into the politics that had been on the wane.

------

160. SMITH, MATTHEW J. "The Power of the Crown." In *Liberty, Fraternity, Exile: Haiti and Jamaica after Emancipation*, 181–95. University of North Carolina Press, 2014. http://www.jstor.org/stable/10.5149/9781469617985_smith.14.

27

LET IT ALL GO

THE 12TH PRESIDENT of Haiti emerged as one of the most consequential political figures of his time. Pierre Theoma Boisrond-Canal[161] was born in Les Cayes in 1832 he began his career in the military and served under the administration of Géffrard. He retired from the army in 1867 and became a farmer. He entered politics in 1870 and was elected senator. He spoke up against the loan contracted by the Domingue government and was seen as a political opponent by the de facto ruler of Haiti, Septimus Rameau. He sought and received asylum in the home of the U.S. ambassador before his exile in Jamaica.

---

161. Dorsainvil, Dr. J. C. "Manuel Histoire D'Haiti" Editions Henri Deschamps; Portus Principis, 15 July 1934

As a member of the Liberal party, he joined other political exiles in Jamaica. The head of the party Boyer-Bazelais was a strong personality whose tactics and positions alienated certain members of the Liberal party. There arose a schism pitting Boisrond-Canal against Boyer-Bazelais. Boisrond-Canal replaced Domingue as provisional president after the ouster of Domingue.

Boisrond-Canal, an astute and effective politician restored parliamentary democracy as had been practiced under the Constitution of 1867. The Liberal Party had a majority in the parliament. The Bazelais faction was in the majority. The Nationalist party (discredited at that time on account of the actions of its leader and founder Septimus Rameau) was in the minority and allied with the Canal faction of the Liberal Party. There was strong opposition in the parliament led by the same party as that of the government. Unfortunately, the Liberal Party was split, and the Nationalist party was also in opposition to the Liberals.

The restoration of the constitutional order and with it the exercise of power by the legislature resulted in much deadlock. The Liberal majority faction opposed the initiatives of the government, and the Nationalists opposed the Liberals. Historians of this period have used a phrase uttered by Boisron-Canal in response to comments about the lack of order and the fact that nothing of note was being achieved. He is said to have responded "Lese grennen" loosely translated as "just let it all go." Said derisively, it was meant to account for the fact that his opponents would not allow his government to get anything done.

Because of his even temper and easygoing nature, Boisrond-Canal adopted the "lese grennen" attitude[162] in contrast to the prior government that sought to eliminate its opponents. While not much was achieved because of the parliamentary deadlock led by the majority Liberals, there was still something worth noting. Haitians were politically free to oppose the government without being killed, persecuted or hounded into exile. The competing parties debated and argued in parliament as they vied to lead the country.

The fact that the constitution was upheld, and that political opposition did not result in an immediate death sentence or exile was an accomplishment of sorts. Such had happened so infrequently in our history. Like Nissage Sage before him, Boisrond-Canal gave political breathing space to the citizens. This was another all too brief interlude of political freedom in our country's first hundred years. This relative freedom

---

162. ibid

came about because of the tolerant attitude of the president along with strong political personalities that forged a counterweight to the power of the executive.[163] In this time, the legislative branch played an important role in the politics of the country.

But the political tensions that defined the Boisrond-Canal administration led to growing frictions. The elections of 1879 were orderly and free leading to the defeat of the Bazelais faction's majority in the parliament. The Nationalist and the Canalist Liberals banded together and held a majority of the chamber. The Liberals, formerly in the majority were not reconciled to these results. After a particularly tumultuous session of the legislature, shots were fired and Boyer-Bazelais and his partisans withdrew from the legislature and revolted. The unfortunate attempt to overturn the election results led to the squelching of the insurrection. Boirond-Canal was not supported by most in his Liberal party and also by the Nationalists. Given this weak hand, he resigned in July 1879 with a year left to his term in office.

Some describe the story of Haiti as a succession of dictatorships. The examples left by Boisrond-Canal, Nissage Saget, and

---

163. Dorsainvil, Dr. J. C. "Manuel Histoire D'Haiti" Editions Henri Deschamps; Portus Principis, 15 July 1934

Alexandre Pétion belie that assertion. Some who advance this distorted view of our history do so out of misunderstanding or malice. The malicious observers of our history were plentiful in the 19th century as the slavocrats sought to sully our reputation at every turn. They needed to justify their onerous enslavement of innocent people. Thus, they asserted that those of African descent were incapable of self-government, highlighting those instances of brutality and repression to prove their point.

Those who suggest Haiti has been governed by a succession of brutal dictators fail to honor the valiant among us who advocated for political liberty and paid for it with their very lives. In every generation, good people sacrificed life and limb to fight for a better vision of our nation and to bring about freedom.

While we acknowledge that for the most part, we have been governed by dictators, not all were brutal. Some dictators were such because they governed extra constitutionally not because their regimes were brutal or repressive. One must distinguish between those who ruled by fear, violence and oppression versus those who brutally put down violent uprisings and revolts whose sole purpose was to replace one dictator with another. Certain of our presidents cannot be described as benevolent, and yet did not harass all their opponents.

These are more than just nuances. Such distinctions meant life or death to many individuals. We celebrate the administrations of Nissage Saget and Boisrond-Canal for governing within the framework of the constitution then in place. They shared power with the legislative branch and worked with their opponents. Opportunities to exercise raw power abounded, but their even-handed temperament and sense of respect for their fellow citizens stayed their hand.[164]

These presidencies were no doubt the exception but arose out of our political culture and traditions just as much as the oppressive tyrants. We produced great orators and parliamentarians and leaders who did not occupy the executive branch. There was freedom enough for opposing points of view to be heard and expressed, and for all sorts of people to assemble without fear of retribution. Our history is much more than a long succession of dictatorships and brutal repression.

---

164. Dorsainvil, Dr. J. C. "Manuel Histoire D'Haiti" Editions Henri Deschamps; Portus Principis, 15 July 1934

28

A DICTATOR WITH A PLAN

L YSIUS SALOMON was born in les Cayes to a prominent and influential family who were active in politics.[165] His father was among those who led an armed insurrection against the government of Rivière-Hérard in 1843. This faction was defeated, and Salomon was forced into exile. Salomon's father was again implicated in another insurrection, this time against Géffrard. He along with the other conspirators were executed in 1863. As the scion of a politically powerful family Lysius Salomon did not come from humble origins. Quite the contrary he and his kin were part of the political, social and economic elite of the country.

---

165. Nicholls, David. "The Wisdom of Salomon: Myth or Reality?" *Journal of Interamerican Studies and World Affairs* 20, no. 4 (1978): 377–92. https://doi.org/10.2307/165442.

He rose to become a Senator under Riche. Under Soulouqe, he became minister of finance. While minister, he imposed taxes and controls over exports in coffee and cotton through the monopoly of the state enterprises. Consequently, smuggling proliferated to the detriment of the economy. After the fall of Soulouque, Salomon was exiled and lived in Paris. Even there he exercised considerable influence over Haitian politics. His family had a base of support in the south and successive governments were reluctant to allow him back from his exile. At times he was called on to serve as Haitian minister to London and Paris. On other occasions he was out of favor and was a simple exile. In either event, those in power considered it prudent to keep him away from Haiti.

He spent a long 20 years in exile.[166] He read and traveled widely and rose to a level of sophistication that few Haitians had achieved. He was an intellectual force and widely considered among the most capable of his generation. At the age of 64, his moment had arrived. He was full of energy, vigor and had a vision for the modernization of Haiti. He returned to Haiti with his French wife, Florentine Potiez Salomon, and

---

166. Sheller, Mimi (2000). Democracy After Slavery: Black Publics and Peasant Radicalism in Haiti and Jamaica. University Press of Florida. p. 129–130. ISBN 0-8130-1883-8.

their daughter Ida (who was to become one of the most celebrated female poets that Haiti has ever produced).

Salomon was virulently opposed by the Liberals who led a rebellion in the city of St. Marc. The response on the part of the government was to round up anyone suspected of collusion with the Liberal leaders Boyer-Bazelais and Edmond Paul. The uprising was put down. But in contradiction to the constitution that prohibited capital punishment, scores of opponents were executed.

Another attempt to overthrow Salomon was led by Boyer-Bazelais himself, and several southern cities such as Miragoane, Jèrèmie, and Jacmel revolted against the government. The government's strategy to defeat the insurgents was to isolate them in the cities that they controlled. This strategy succeeded in defeating the rebellion, with the rebels succumbing to starvation and illness. Boyer-Bazelais in a weakened state perished from dysentery along with many of his partisans. Those rebels who survived were summarily executed. The Salomon government dealt brutally thus standing in contrast to the tolerance and comparative benevolence shown by Nissage Saget.

But there were tangible signs of progress under Salomon.[167] The Banque Nationale was established. Repayment of the country's debt to France was resumed. Haiti joined the International Postal Union, and our first postage stamps were issued. The country became connected via cable to Jamaica, Cuba and North America. The medical school was restructured, and more resources were devoted to education. Teachers were brought from France to enhance the level and quality of education. Numerous primary schools were opened.

This was a government with a real plan to achieve progress. The military was reformed, and a French military mission helped to raise the professionalization of the army. New government buildings were introduced including a Presidential Palace. The growth of agriculture was encouraged by the reduction of taxes on exports of cotton and coffee. Agriculture reform was introduced to allow for those who cultivated land to acquire title to these plots.

As his seven-year presidential term neared its end, Salomon pressured the legislature to amend the constitution to allow him to remain in office for another seven years. Though

---

167. Nicholls, David. "The Wisdom of Salomon: Myth or Reality?" *Journal of Interamerican Studies and World Affairs* 20, no. 4 (1978): 377–92. https://doi.org/10.2307/165442.

initiatives had been undertaken by the government to modernize the nation, there was a sense of fatigue with Salomon. Salomon was reelected to another seven-year term leading to an uprising in 1888.

Led by General Seide Telemaque, Cap-Haitien rebelled. By this time Salomon was deeply unpopular and besieged on all sides. The end came when General Herard Laforest, the commander of the Port-au-Prince garrison, also rebelled. Losing all control, Salomon left Haiti and returned to France where he died not much later in October 1888.

Salomon among the most qualified of our presidents, came to office with a plan to modernize. While in office he implemented many changes to move the country forward.[168] The service of our debt and the funds needed to put down the manifold rebellions left the treasury in distress. The government was forced to issue paper money and thereby weakening the economy.

From the first, Salomon was virulently opposed by the considerable political force of the Liberals. He defeated the Liberal led uprisings and did so in a brutal manner that shocked public opinion. Unlike some predecessors he failed to exercise restraint and executed his opponents. He repressed the

---

168. ibid

opposition, and the legislature was reduced to a rubber stamp. Salomon's government severely reduced the political freedoms that Haitians had fought so hard to obtain.

29

AGE of PROGRESS

U PON SALOMON'S DEPARTURE a provisional government was constituted with Boisrond-Canal as president. Regional divisions and passions were in play, and the major political figures were Generals Francois Denys Légitime and Seide Thelemaque. Légitime led the west and south while Thelemaque's support came from the north. Each with troops under his command vied for power. From the point of view of the northerners, the past three presidents came from the south. They felt it was their turn to have a president.

The issue came to arms. In the ensuing conflict, General Thelemaque lost his life, and the western/southern faction defeated the northerners. The remaining northern leaders such as General Florvil Hyppolite withdrew to the north.

The legislature elected General Légitime[169] president of Haiti. Though the representatives of the north were absent, nonetheless there was a quorum and Légitime duly elected.

Légitime did not last long as president. His election was rejected by the north who formed its revolutionary committee led by General Hyppolite and included such political heavyweights as Anténor Firmin. Légitime was besieged from the north and there were armed movements in the south against him. General Merisier Jeannis led his troops against Légitime. The combined pressure and the defection of some his key supporters led Légitime to leave in August 1889. He had barely been president and thus unable to leave his mark on the national scene. The country was bitterly divided, and Legitime was not strong enough politically or militarily to stay in office. He had to resign.

FLORVIL HYPPOLITE 1889–96

As was the custom by then, a provisional government was established. The leading figures included Generals Nord Alexis, Florvil Hyppolite[170] and Antenor Firmin. A new constitution

---

169. Arthur Rouzier. *Les belles figures de l'intelligentsia jérémienne.* Publisher unknown (1986), p. 55.

170. "The Late President Hyppolite of Haiti". *The Chautauquan. XXIII: 238. May 1896*

was adopted, and Florvil Hyppolite was elected to a seven-year term as the new president. Hyppolite, a military man, valued discipline and order. His disciplined troops allowed him to exert considerable political influence.

Born in Cap-Haitien in 1827, he entered public life under Soulouque. He did not appear on the national political scene again until the overthrow of Salomon by Legitime. Hyppolite was among the northern generals under the leadership of General Seide Thelemaque. The events of 1889 leading to Legitime's departure brought Hyppolite to office.

MOLE ST. NICOLAS

During the uprising that led to the departure of Legitime, the United States had provided munitions and transport to Hyppolite's troops. Hyppolite thus came to office perceived as beholden to the United States. For its part the United States anticipated that the Hyppolite government would be a willing partner in acquiring the strategically important Mole St Nicolas, an an ideal base to monitor naval traffic in the region. A fleet of U.S. naval ships entered Port-au-Prince harbor in 1891 to negotiate the terms for Mole St. Nicolas.[171]

---

171. Léger, Jacques Nicolas (1907). *Haiti, Her History and Her Detractors.* New York; Washington: The Neale Pub. Co. pp. 245–247.

The reaction of the local population was immediately hostile. Ceding any part of Haiti's territory to a foreign power was anathema. In fact, the constitution of 1889 expressly forbade giving up territory. Antenor Firmin, the minister of foreign affairs, defused the situation by pointing out that admiral who headed the fleet did not have the right diplomatic papers authorizing him to lead such a mission. In the end, we were able to keep our territory and not allow a foreign power a base on our soil.

In the first year of his mandate, Hyppolite declared an amnesty allowing those exiled to return home. Antenor Firmin[172] was both the minister of finance and foreign affairs and was an able administrator who was proactive, honest and restored much needed order. Firmin, among Haiti's most renowned intellectuals, also became one of the best ministers of any government. He played a major role in the success of the Hyppolite administration.

In this administration there was a greater degree of free expression and restraint. The legislative branch was allowed to function without interference. The press was free to criticize the government, and the average citizens could conduct their

---

172. Bernasconi, Robert. (2008). 'A Haitian in Paris: Anténor Firmin as a Philosopher Against Racism'. Patterns of Prejudice 42.4–5: 365–383.

affairs without interference from the government. Prior governments tended to oppression when dealing with opponents.

But there were uprisings and attempts by the opposition to overthrow the government.[173] After one such attempt the president, known to have quite a temper, flew into a rage and sought revenge on the perpetrators and his perceived enemies. For days there was terror and apprehension. But having thought the better of it, Hyppolite declared a general amnesty.

The instances of amnesty were rare, and were even more so after an attempt to overthrow the government. Few presidents displayed such restraint toward the opposition. Hyppolite joined the few and rare presidents Nissage Sage and Boisrond-Canal who allowed opponents the space to operate without fear of losing their lives.

Hyppolite introduced the ministry of public works to improve the infrastructure of the country. Public works involving telegraphy, telephone, cable as well as the wharf, ports and the public markets were initiated. No government did more to develop our infrastructure. The construction of the public ministries building (started under Salomon) was completed. Haiti even participated in the World's Fair of Chicago in 1893.

---

173. Dorsainvil, Dr. J. C. "Manuel Histoire D'Haiti" Editions Henri Deschamps; Portus Principis, 15 July 1934

In 1896, General Merisier Jeannis led a revolt in his southern stronghold, attacking the public places in Jacmel. Hyppolite personally led the government' s response to this latest attempt to overthrow his government. Against the advice of his closest confidants and even his personal physician, Hyppolite got on his horse leading his troops south. He got as far as the city of Leogane (not far from Port-au-Prince) fell off of horse and died of a heart attack. Like Pétion before him, he died in office. He wasn't overthrown and did not get to complete his term. He left behind a legacy of public works, and a firm yet benevolent rule over the country.[174] He ranks among our best presidents. Unlike many an occupant of that office, he left the nation in a markedly better position than when he entered the presidency.

TIRESIAS SIMON SAM 1896–1902

Within a week of the death of President Hyppolite, the National Assembly gathered and elected Tiresias Simon Sam the new president of Haiti to serve a seven-year term.[175] Sworn

---

174. Dorsainvil, Dr. J. C. "Manuel Histoire D'Haiti" Editions Henri Deschamps; Portus Principis, 15 July 1934

175. ibid

in on March 31, 1896, he had previously served as the minister of war under Hyppolite. The Sam administration was in many respects a continuation of the prior government, thus giving the country much needed continuity. Antenor Firmin served as minister of finance and Solon Menos was the minister of foreign relations. These political heavyweights also served under Hyppolite. For a second consecutive administration there was a role for powerful politicians other than the president to exercise authority on behalf of the executive branch. Competent administrators maintained a reputation for probity and efficiency.

The government focused on infrastructure such as the railroads to connect the major cities of the country to the capital. The tramway service was restored, and the construction of the courthouse completed. All were well received and helped toward the nation's continued development.

In 1897, Haiti was yet again the victim of gunboat diplomacy on the part of the German empire asserting its presence in the region. It began with a criminal matter in which a German citizen named Luders was involved. Haitian justice deemed him guilty, thus creating a diplomatic incident when the German charge d'affaires escalated the matter and demanded the immediate release of Luders along with the firing of the judges and policemen involved in the matter. Luders was indeed released and left for Germany.

The Germans did not let the matter rest. Months later, two German gunboats landed in Port-au-Prince's harbor, and the commandant delivered an ultimatum to the government. The humiliating terms included paying an indemnity to Luders, a 21-gun salute to the German gunboats and a letter of apology addressed to the German government. The ultimatum was delivered with the threat of immediate bombardment of the capital.

The government with but hours to deliberate, gave in to the humiliating conditions imposed by Germany. The Germans left. The result was a fatal blow to the prestige of the Sam government. By capitulating the government lost its popularity and legitimacy in many eyes.[176] Opponents argued that the presidential mandate should expire in 1902 rather than in 1903 as previously understood. The basis of this argument was a mere technicality, but it gained momentum. Rather than fight to hang on to power, or aggressively challenge his

---

176. Dorsainvil, Dr. J. C. "Manuel Histoire D'Haiti" Editions Henri Deschamps; Portus Principis, 15 July 1934

opponents, Sam chose to resign. He lasted six years in office and was not overthrown.

The governments of Hyppolite and Sam provided the nation with stability and a consistent policy favoring investments in infrastructure and the general development of the country. From 1889–1902 the country was governed responsibly with governments that exercised restraint when dealing with the opposition. Haiti achieved measurable progress in those years. Construction of buildings, roads, bridges, telegraph, telephone, ports, public markets, railways, and a tram service constituted the visible signs of progress. There was political stability, as major players in the Hyppolite administration, Antenor Firmin for example, were major players in the Sam government. The administration of the country was in capable hands. There were no scandals or allegations of corruption. No civil wars or internal insurrections marked the period.

Indeed, there was peace and a measure of prosperity (within the context of our history). These two successive administrations achieved what many others failed to deliver to the nation: progress. Moreover, that progress was achieved without the political repression so common in the exercise of power in our history. These governments allowed Haiti to stand alongside the sister republics of the hemisphere and participate in the Chicago World Fair of 1893. Diplomatic relations were maintained with the major powers as the era of diplomatic isolation had ended. Haiti was no longer viewed as the pariah nation that was anathema to the slavocracy of the early to mid-19th century.

30

A LEADING LIGHT

After the departure of President Sam, a provisional government was put in place with Boisrond-Canal as president. Again, he answered the call to serve his country. No other former presidents in our history have been called upon to serve again, even as interim, to organize a new government.[177] This speaks volumes about the esteem in which he was held. The task of the provisional government was to organize new elections for the legislature. The man of the moment who inspired the youth at that time was Antenor Firmin who was widely admired for his prior experience in

____

177. Dorsainvil, Dr. J. C. "Manuel Histoire D'Haiti" Editions Henri Deschamps; Portus Principis, 15 July 1934

government, intellect and probity. He had served ably and was considered the leading candidate to become the next President.

Others presented their candidacy, among them included General Pierre Nord Alexis, a well-known national figure involved in high level politics for decades. Moreover, he controlled an army that was the linchpin of his support. By June the tensions among the partisans of the candidates had reached a boiling point. Supporters of Firmin and Nord Alexis were openly fighting in Cap-Haitien. Firmin and his supporters withdrew to Gonaives, and his supporters rallied to the cause.

The Firministe party abandoned Port-au-Prince to be with the candidate in Gonaives, thus leaving the capital to the political machinations of those who opposed Firmin. One by one the other candidates fell in line with Nord Alexis, and the matter would be resolved by the force of arms. A civil war ensued. Firmin's camp had among its supporters the charismatic Admiral Hammerton Killick who had the gunship Crete-a-Pierrot under his control. This same ship was used to transport munitions to the Firmin camp in Gonaives.

The provisional government who by that time was under the control of Nord Alexis enlisted the aid of a German ship[178] the

178. Simpson, Lloyd P. "THE GERMAN-HAITIAN NAVAL CLASH OF 1902." *Warship International* 3, no. 3 (1966): 216–216. http://www.jstor.org/stable/44887305.

Panther to capture the Crete-a-Pierrot and reclaim the arms and munitions on board the ship. The Panther arrived in the harbor of Gonaives, and Admiral Killick quickly recognized that his ship was no match for the *Panther*. Rather than submit, he ordered his crew to disembark. He was left all alone except for his doctor, Coles.

Wrapping himself in the Haitian flag, he blew up the ship. Rather than submit to a foreign power, and believing in his cause he offered his life.[179] By this singular act of bravery, the admiral has been recognized as one of our national heroes. This transcendent act recalled the sacrifices that our forefathers were willing to bear to secure our independence. Admiral Killick reminded his generation of the qualities that helped us become an independent people. He is a celebrated symbol of our freedom and of our willingness to die rather than submit.

In the end, the loss of the munitions on the Crete-a-Pierrot left the Firministe fighters bereft of much-needed arms and munitions. They were defeated and unable to carry on. Nord Alexis and his troops entered Port-au-Prince in December. His army declared him president of Haiti, with ratification by the legislature soon to follow.

---

179. Nicholls, David (1996). *From Dessalines to Duvalier: Race, Colour, and National Independence in Haiti*. Rutgers University Press. p. 140

ANTENOR FIRMIN

Born in 1850 in Cap-Haitien, he died in 1911 in St. Thomas at age of 60. Among the leading lights of his generation, he was known as a philosopher, anthropologist, journalist and statesmen. He is best known for his book l'Egalité des Races Humaines which was published in 1885 as a rebuttal to the book written by Count Arthur de Robineau entitled Essai sur l'Inegalité des Races Humaines.[180] Gobineau sought to assert the superiority of the Aryan race and the inferiority of peoples of color. In his book, Firmin took the opposite position and argued forcefully that "all men are endowed with the same qualities and faults without distinction of color or anatomical form. The races are equal."

Firmin made an important contribution to the debate around racial equality. His voice was certainly one of the few at that time, to make the counterpoint about the equality of all human beings regardless of ethnic origin.

Haitians owe a debt to him for defending what we have known and experienced, that no race or ethnic group is superior to others. At a time of burgeoning imperialism, colonialism, and segregation his was a lonely but authentic voice.

---

180. Fluehr-Lobban, Carolyn (September 2000). "Antenor Firmin: Haitian Pioneer of Anthropology." American Anthropologist. 102 (3): 449–466.

He was a free man whose ancestors had thrown the shackles of slavery by themselves. He was able to speak for them, those of his generation and for us who followed. In the end his arguments prevailed.

Haitians are proud to have been the ones answering the faulty arguments of the racists by word and deed. The book written by Firmin is one of the clear examples of Haitians engaging in the debate around race and freedom. Ours was a lone voice present in the literary halls and salons of the then intellectual capital of the world, Paris. We defended and promoted the idea of equality amongst all human beings.

Firmin, from a working class background in Cap-Haitian, was a brilliant student who studied law and accounting. He served in the Customs Office and worked as a clerk in private business. Leaving those positions to teach Greek, Latin and French. He joined the Liberal Party, and President Salomon forced him into exile as a diplomat in France. Powerful and talented political opponents were often shipped to a diplomatic posting overseas and away from the political fray.

While in Paris, Firmin was admitted to the prestigious and exclusive Société d'Anthropologie de Paris. He rose to speak out against racialist ideas. He is likely to have been the first recognized anthropologist of African descent.

Firmin was among those who founded the idea of Pan-Africanism[181] to combat colonialism then ravaging Africa. He organized the first Pan-African Conference in 1900 that launched the Pan-African movement. Alongside this work, he conceived of a Caribbean Confederation encompassing the union of Cuba, Haiti, the Dominican Republic, Jamaica and Puerto Rico. His sought to create political and social unity throughout the Caribbean.

As a statesman, he served as minister of finance and foreign affairs under President Sam and minister of foreign affairs under Florvil Hyppolite. He helped maintain Mole St. Nicholas as part of Haiti despite repeated pressure from the United States to use it as a naval base. As finance minister he distinguished himself by the efficient administration of the nation's finances.

As recounted earlier, he failed in his attempts to achieve the highest position in the land, that of president. His failed attempt at the presidency was brutally defeated by the forces of Nord Alexis. After Alexis was overthrown, he was sent to London as ambassador the British Empire. His last attempt at the presidency came in 1910 and again met with defeat. He

---

181. Magloire-Danton, Gerarde (2005). "Antenor Firmin and Jean Price-Mars: Revolution, Memory, Humanism." *Small Axe.* 9 (2): 150–170.

went into exile in St. Thomas where he died shortly thereafter in 1911.[182] One can only wonder what would have been had Firmin risen to the presidency.

Notwithstanding his failure to reach the presidency, he left an indelible mark. His work as an anthropologist is more appreciated today than in his time. He remains one of the leading Haitians of our first century and stands as an example of what we Haitians can achieve. His influence and contributions have outpaced those of who held the office of president.

---

182. Dorsainvil, Dr. J. C. "Manuel Histoire D'Haiti" Editions Henri Deschamps; Portus Principis, 15 July 1934

31

CENTENNIAL

Born in Cap-Haitien in 1820, Nord Alexis was 82 when he ascended to the presidency.[183] His father was a high ranking official in the service of Henri Christophe and his mother was an illegitimate daughter of Christophe. Thus, his grandfather was once King of Haiti. He joined the army in 1830 and served as the aide-de-camp to his father-in-law president Jean-Louis Pierrot. He had a long career in the political life of the nation. He was in the opposition under Salomon and given control of the military in the northern region under Hyppolite.

---

183. Dorsainvil, Dr. J. C. "Manuel Histoire D'Haiti" Editions Henri Deschamps; Portus Principis, 15 July 1934

In the struggle for the presidency, Alexis allied with Boisrond Canal and the U.S. He pledged to foster U.S. interests in the Caribbean. In return the U.S. led a naval blockade of the ports controlled by Firmin. Alexis prevailed but left a trail of blood and bitter opposition to his regime.

Alexis hailed from a generation of political and military leaders that had faded from the scene. His contemporaries had long been replaced by a new generation of leaders. His was the generation of the general politician who led an army to take the presidency. That was no longer the profile of those most prominent in national leadership. Firmin represented another path to national leadership, where the ascent to the presidency was not based solely on the force of arms. Alexis was motivated by the veneration of our elders, the founders of our nation, and in maintaining our independence.

THE MATTER OF CONSOLIDATION

In 1903 the government formed a commission to investigate charges of corruption in the prior administration. The matter in question was the negotiation of the loans contracted by the Sam administration. In point of fact, there were valid concerns that officials had benefited from the loans at the expense of the nation. This initiative was without precedent in the annals of our history, the investigation of former officials and private citizens for acts of corruption. The desire to address the issue of corruption was widely accepted.

But the Alexis administration used the investigation to pursue its opponents. Thus, the legitimacy of the process came into question. It was seen for what it came to be, a witch-hunt and cudgel to neutralize opponents.

In 1908, Nord Alexis proclaimed himself "President for Life." This led to an insurrection by the Firministe opposition led by General Jean Jumeau. This rebellion was defeated, and conspiracies abounded. The opposition was determined to overthrow Alexis. One such conspiracy had at its head the celebrated poet Massillon Coicou, another Firmin supporter. The twenty conspirators included Coicou and his brothers were executed.[184] This led to hardening the opposition to Alexis, rendering his government even more unpopular.

Another rebellion, led this time by General Antoine Simon from the south defeated the troops loyal to the government. Simon's army marched towards Port-au-Prince. With his fate sealed Alexis sought the protection of the French ambassador.

---

184. Dorsainvil, Dr. J. C. "Manuel Histoire D'Haiti" Editions Henri Deschamps; Portus Principis, 15 July 1934

Taken to Kingston, Jamaica, Alexis left as an unpopular president who failed to leave a mark.

NATIONAL ANTHEM

On January 1, 1904, our centennial was celebrated in Gonaives,[185] where our independence was first proclaimed. In preparation for the celebration, a National Association for the Centennial was established to direct the festivities. A competition was established to compose a national anthem. The famed poet Justin L'Herisson won for his potent and vibrant words that harken to our forefathers. The musical score came next, the composition submitted by Nicolas Geffrard was selected. Lastly the name chosen for the anthem was "La Dessalienne" in honor of our leading founder and emperor Jean-Jacques Dessalines.

The new anthem was immediately seen as a powerful symbol of our hard-won liberty. The verses call upon us to remember our forefathers, homeland and to walk together in unity:

For the country, for the ancestors, let us march,
  let us march united.
Let there be no traitors in our ranks!

---

185. ibid

Let us be masters of our soil.

United let us march for the Country, for the ancestors.

For the forefathers, for the country, let us toil joyfully.

When the field is fertile our soul strengthens.

Let us toil joyfully for our forbearers, for our country.

For the country and the forefathers, let us train our sons,

    free strong and prosperous.

We shall always be brothers.

Let us train our sons for the country and for the

    forefathers.

For the forefathers, for the country.

Oh God of the valiant!

Take our rights and our life under your infinite protection,

    Oh God of the valiant!

For the forefathers for the country.

For the flag, for the country to die is a glorious deed!

Our past cries out to us: Have a seasoned soul!

To die is a glorious deed, for the flag, for the country.

The verses of our anthem sum up our history and our aspirations. Introduced at the celebration our first centennial, they inspire us today. They remind us of the spirit that propelled the most improbable outcome, slaves overthrowing their oppressors to live free. They also tell us that giving our lives for our country and the forefathers who brought us our liberty is indeed a most glorious deed. That is the spirit which won us our independence and allowed us to maintain it for a century.

This story that has not been told often enough. This is our narrative. This is the spirit that will renew our nation and our people.

POSTSCRIPT

This narrative ends with the celebration of the first hundred years of our independence. That period coincides with the beginning of the 20th century and the age of progress. The European empires dominated the world and were playing the "Great Game" as if the nations, peoples and regions of the world were theirs to master. Our small nation was for most of the first century a single and solitary voice that stood for the proposition, that all men are created equal. Humankind is one and the same. The right to enslave was a horror and stain on all of humanity.

At our hundredth anniversary, we had outlasted the enslavers. They were relegated to the dustbin of history. In

North America, the American Civil War was the bloodiest and costliest of the efforts to eradicate slavery. In the other powers, slavery ended by decrees of emancipation and by the efforts of moralizers such as William Wilberforce in the United Kingdom. Even in mighty Russia the absolutist Czar Alexander II freed the serfs from their bondage. The last bastion of slavery was Brazil and in 1888 the "Golden Law" was decreed under the rule of Emperor Dom Pedro in Brazil.

It took almost all of the 19th century for slavery to be universally accepted as abhorrent and treated as an antiquated vestige of the past. The economic advantages that came with slavery were not abolished. Though laws and decrees were passed, those who had been enslaved continued to face exploitation and lived under conditions not much better than their prior state. But the end of slavery did bring to those former victims of that heinous system legal rights and the recognition that all were equal before the law. In the U.S. the separate-but-equal, segregation system became the way to continue the oppression and economic exploitation of those formerly enslaved.

Overall those who were formerly enslaved all throughout the world were given or granted a form of legal emancipation, meaning that no human being could treat another as chattel. It is important to note that the only instance of the formerly enslaved taking up arms and freeing themselves from bondage happened in Haiti. The enslavers around the world conspired to keep that from ever happening again. Different formulas in different locations succeeded for generations. We Haitians were exceptions to the rule.

Those who tire of our affirming this fact must bow before the reality that no other rebellion of the formerly enslaved ever succeeded. In modern times none ever came close. One must go back to ancient Rome and Spartacus to find a comparable event. Our first hundred years ended on January 1, 1904. The world did not celebrate with Haiti. We savored our centennial, but its meaning was lost on the rest of the world. We were true to the sacrifices made by our forefathers. We remained free and independent.

Upon reflection the first century meant that the life of the average Haitian was better than that of the enslaved, but more could have been achieved. Political freedom was enjoyed for all too brief interludes. Those periods depended upon the mood and dictates of those wielding power. The range of political freedom stretched from the terror under Soulouque to the firm hand of Hyppolite to the benevolence of Nissage Saget, and Boisrond Canal.

Painting the story of the first hundred years with the broad brush of dictatorship, ignores the fact that our political history, though marked by instability, was not always one of repression. At times the legislative branch was predominant, wielding power to the annoyance of the executive branch. This happened during the period of the Liberal ascendency with political leaders such as Boyer-Bazelais leading the way to restrain the executive branch.

That period also saw the emergence of the Nationaliste Party as a counterweight to the Liberal Party. Two slogans were adopted by the parties to rally their supporters." Power to the greatest number" affirmed the Nationalistes, while the Liberals advocated for "Power to those most capable." Political parties vied for power. There was freedom for those in opposition to assemble and express their points of view.

Unfortunately, such was not the norm throughout our first century. The politics can be defined as resting in the hands of the supreme leader.

At times that leader was crowned emperor (Jacques 1er and Faustin 1er) and king, Henri. This concentration of power in the hands of the monarch eventually led to despotism. Those closest to the monarchs ultimately betrayed them. Violent insurrections led to the tragic deaths of our first emperor and only king.

The narrative here can energize the children of the Haitian nation who have not learned our history as we have taught it to ourselves. This condensed tour d'horizon is meant to whet the appetite and stimulate greater interest and discussion around that oft overlooked part of our history. Great things were accomplished that have not been celebrated nearly enough. Most importantly when viewed by our lens we can conclude that Haitians are capable of great things. In fact, great and important things were accomplished after independence. This narrative also seeks to highlight the fact of a hundred years of total independence, free of foreign occupation or other compromises to our freedom and sovereignty. To have survived a full century in the face of opposition and enemies is an extraordinary achievement.

By recounting the story of our first century this author seeks to encourage others to tell and retell the story in our words for everyone to remember.

POOR HAITI

The republic of Haiti, occupies the western third of the island of Hispaniola, is a land often described as the poorest nation in the Western Hemisphere. This assertion has defined a nation wracked by political instability, corruption, and natural disasters. Haiti evinces sympathy from those well-meaning servants of God who willingly give of their time and talent to demonstrate compassion and empathy to the least of their brethren. The international aid workers and those operating the Non-Governmental Organizations (NGOs) have all helped define how Haiti is viewed. Poor Haiti. The poorest country in the Western Hemisphere and the object of pity. Time to replace that pity with respect.

The people of Haiti have been seen as long suffering and heroic in the face of obstacles that would have bested other peoples. Haitians are energetic, motivated, innovative, resilient, spiritual, artistic, warm, expressive, passionate, proud, stubborn and sometimes unable to work together for their common good. This people has spread to neighboring countries in circumstances demonstrating both courage and desperation. Once outside of Haiti, the positive attributes are allowed free reign, and they contribute meaningfully wherever they land: in the Bahamas, Canada, the Dominican Republic, France and the United States.

We have survived ecological devastation, flash floods, hurricanes and finally the "big one" earthquake of the century. Haitians have had much to overcome just to survive.

Few are willing to help sort out the mess that Haiti has become. The UN has terminated its protectorate mission. The droves of helpers who came to "build back Haiti better" after the earthquake have swallowed their disillusionment and departed. Theirs were but steps in the sand that left no permanent tracks. The international donor community now is suffering another bout of Haiti fatigue.

On the ground, the country is mismanaged and politically unstable. Armed gangs are terrorizing the population, while those who govern have demonstrated a stunning lack of concern for their fellow citizens coupled with a rapacious appetite for corruption. The public sector is weak, at best ineffective. The government is paralyzed by internecine struggles between the executive and legislative branches. There is no articulated and agreed upon consensus regarding the rule of law and democratic principles. The political class has operated with the leitmotif of "ote toi que je m'y mette" loosely translated as "step aside so that I can take over."

At times, Haiti's political and economic elites have been referred to as MRE (Morally Repugnant Elite). There is a grossly unequal distribution of wealth. The few who are economically prosperous control a disproportionate portion of the formal and informal economy. The traffic in drugs and other illegal activity represents another stain on the fabric of the nation. The diaspora Haitians (those living overseas) provide remittances that provide a ballast to alleviate some of the misery. The penury faced by most Haitians saps their morale, ambition and willingness to sacrifice to create a better future.

No wonder that those who look at Haiti from the outside conclude that the place is a mess. The narrative can be summed up with these words: Poor Haiti!

I have written this book to challenge that narrative. There is much more to Haiti than the "poorest country" moniker. I have retold our story in our words to prove that our forefathers overcame obstacles far more daunting than what we face today. By looking back and celebrating our past, we can be inspired to believe in ourselves yet again. Haiti is possible! Haiti will rise! *L'UNION FAIT LA FORCE!*

ACKNOWLEDGMENTS

My interest in Haitian history was passed down to me by my father whose passion for this topic was contagious. I remember him describing in great detail the agony that Toussaint suffered in the cold at the Fort de Joux. That night I couldn't sleep. Once we visited Haiti he took us to the pont rouge where Dessalines was assassinated and acted out the scene. Haitian history is in my DNA. My mother's family the Chatelain's are great storytellers who regaled me with the stories of our past. To them I owe a great debt of gratitude. They infused in me a love of our history and a desire to share it. Writing this was important so that I could share this passion with my children Gaëlle, Remy, Chloé and Gilles to pass the baton along.

To my dear friend Dave Lawrence who so graciously edited several drafts of this book to make it more concise and direct. He was generous with his time and wrote the introduction. cannot thank you enough.

My daughter Gaëlle has served as editor/research assistant and collaborator. Her assistance with the footnotes and insights on certain passages helped take this effort to whole new level. I am deeply grateful that she chose to spend time on this project with me. It has brought us closer together.

Gilles, my youngest, helped research and find the photographs of the key actors of our first century.

Last but not least to my best friend, soul mate and life partner, Marjorie. You put up with my ramblings and encouraged me every step of the way. This book would not have been written without your support.

To all who will read this book, especially the next generation, please believe in Haiti and never give up on her people.

ABOUT THE AUTHOR

Ghislain Gouraige, fils was born in Port-au-Prince, Haiti and moved with his family to the United States at the age of 8. Though he has spent the bulk of his life living outside the country he has maintained strong ties to his family and native land. He travels annually to Haiti and has been an active contributor to the evolution of the Haitian community in his adopted hometown of Miami. He served as a co-chair of the Haiti Committee of the Greater Miami Chamber of Commerce. He was appointed by then Governor Jeb Bush to the Haiti Advisory Group whose purpose it was to guide the State of Florida in its efforts to help Haiti. He currently serves as the Chair of Ayiti Community Trust which was formed to support and sustain development innovation in Haiti in the areas of civic education, the environment, and entrepreneurship.